# A New World in Our Hearts

**KAIROS**

In ancient Greek philosophy, *kairos* signifies the right time or the "moment of transition." We believe that we live in such a transitional period. The most important task of social science in time of transformation is to transform itself into a force of liberation. Kairos, an editorial imprint of the Anthropology and Social Change department housed in the California Institute of Integral Studies, publishes groundbreaking works in critical social sciences, including anthropology, sociology, geography, theory of education, political ecology, political theory, and history.

Series editor: Andrej Grubačić

**Recent and featured Kairos books:**

*Between Thought and Expression Lies a Lifetime: Why Ideas Matter* by Noam Chomsky and James Kelman

*Mutual Aid: An Illuminated Factor of Evolution* by Peter Kropotkin, illustrated by N.O. Bonzo

*Asylum for Sale: Profit and Protest in the Migration Industry* edited by Siobhán McGuirk and Adrienne Pine

*Building Free Life: Dialogues with Öcalan* edited by International Initiative

*The Art of Freedom: A Brief History of the Kurdish Liberation Struggle* by Havin Guneser

*The Sociology of Freedom: Manifesto of the Democratic Civilization, Volume III* by Abdullah Öcalan

*Facebooking the Anthropocene in Raja Ampat* by Bob Ostertag

*In, Against, and Beyond Capitalism: The San Francisco Lectures* by John Holloway

*Re-enchanting the World: Feminism and the Politics of the Commons* by Silvia Federici

*Practical Utopia: Strategies for a Desirable Society* by Michael Albert

*Autonomy Is in Our Hearts: Zapatista Autonomous Government through the Lens of the Tsotsil Language* by Dylan Eldredge Fitzwater

**For more information visit www.pmpress.org/blog/kairos/**

# A New World in Our Hearts

## Noam Chomsky in Conversation
## with Michael Albert

KAIROS

PM

*A New World in Our Hearts: Noam Chomsky in Conversation with Michael Albert*
Noam Chomsky
© Michael Albert and Valeria Chomsky 2022
Preface © Lydia Sargent 2022
This edition © PM Press 2022

ISBN: 978–1–62963–868–3 (paperback)
ISBN: 978–1–62963–869–0 (hardcover)
ISBN: 978–1–62963–892–8 (ebook)
Library of Congress Control Number: 2020947279

Cover design by John Yates
Layout by briandesign

10 9 8 7 6 5 4 3 2 1

PM Press
PO Box 23912
Oakland, CA 94623
www.pmpress.org

Printed in the USA.

# Contents

# SECTION I
# The Z Sessions

Noam Chomsky is an American linguist, philosopher, cognitive scientist, logician, political commentator, and activist. Sometimes described as the "father of modern linguistics," Chomsky is also a major figure in analytic philosophy. He has spent most of his career at the Massachusetts Institute of Technology, where he is currently institute professor emeritus, and has authored over one hundred books. He has been described as a prominent cultural figure and was voted the "world's top public intellectual" in a 2005 poll.

In February 2010, Z invited Noam Chomsky to spend a day at the Z offices in Woods Hole, Massachusetts, in order to film five sessions on specific topics. The sessions were then transcribed for this book.

The sessions presented here not only expose imperial policies and institutions but also indicate important areas for organizing such as: challenging institutions like capitalism, which demand hierarchical structures of class, race, and gender; and challenging all attempts by the US Empire and its satellite/client states to ignore the will of the population. That is, the sessions point to the need to fight for, reclaim, and develop truly democratic structures and institutions that are counter to the current savage imperialism, oppressive hierarchies, and democracy deficit.

**Lydia Sargent**

# Responsibility of Intellectuals, Scholars, and Journalists

**MICHAEL ALBERT:** Years ago, you wrote an article called "The Responsibility of Intellectuals," so we'll start there and then move on to other topics. The first problem with that title is, what's an intellectual?

**NOAM CHOMSKY:** It's not a term I use very much but it's a term that's used. It refers to people who have sufficient privilege and opportunity so that they're able to speak about affairs with a degree of prestige and authority. They're called intellectuals. A physicist working in a lab, if he's working on something, is not called an intellectual; but if he happens to give a talk, then he's an intellectual. A literary critic who writes about English poets in the late nineteenth century is not an intellectual, but if they happen to write on "the cultural changes that are developing in the modern world," well, okay, then they're an intellectual.

If a shoemaker happens to make a very thoughtful commentary on international affairs or domestic affairs or human relations, she's not usually called an intellectual. So I don't think it's a very meaningful term.

**Nonetheless, what's an intellectual's responsibility?**
You start with the fact that the people designated as intellectuals have privileges, otherwise they wouldn't enter into that category. They have a degree of authority, prestige—justified or not—and these characteristics confer responsibility. Prestige yields opportunity and a degree of credibility. The more opportunity and credibility you have, the more responsibility you have. It's pretty straightforward, like almost everything else.

5

**But what's the nature of the responsibility? If we say that an intellectual is failing to meet their responsibilities, what does that mean?**

We can start with some elementary moral principles that any decent human being ought to accept. For example, one elementary truism is that we should apply to ourselves the same standards we apply to others. So one responsibility of intellectuals is to look at the facts of past and current enemies, the way we've treated them, and look at ourselves, and then ask if we are meeting that elementary moral condition.

So, for example, there happens to be an inquiry going on in England where they're investigating Tony Blair, Jack Straw, and others for background on their involvement in the invasion of Iraq. There's no such inquiry in the United States. In the US, people with power and privilege are immune from any inquiry or discussion. That's part of the prerogative of imperial power. But there is one in England. Well, it's elementary that Blair was involved in direct aggression, and lawyers will try to work their way out of that conclusion, but that's their job.

Look at the Nuremberg proceedings. There's a way to deal with aggression. That's what they were all about: how to deal with acts of aggression. It's the gold standard. For example, the German foreign minister was hanged, and one of the major charges was that he was involved in a preemptive war. He was the foreign minister when Germany invaded Norway because they knew—it was not a secret—that Britain was planning to use a base in Norway to attack Germany. This falls under what's called preemptive war. You carry out military aggression to stop an impending attack on yourself.

**Could you give some examples of people who fulfill their responsibility as intellectuals?**

Let's take Howard Zinn or Eqbal Ahmed or Edward Said. They happened to be close friends; they interacted constantly, so they were kind of a cadre, if you like, of prominent intellectuals, scholars, and activists. Their lives and work were ultimately intertwined, and they dedicated a large part of their lives and work to pursuing elementary moral truisms. So that's a responsible intellectual.

**Can you give a few examples of intellectuals that failed?**

A couple of years ago, the *New York Times* published some Nixon tapes. There was a big battle about releasing them. Henry Kissinger didn't want them released. I think there was a court trial. In any case, they were eventually released. If you look through the tapes—they're mostly gossip, nasty things that Nixon said about somebody, or anti-Semitic remarks—there was one sentence in the article, which, as far as I can see, elicited no comment, except from me and a couple of other people. There was a point where they were talking about the bombing of Cambodia, and Nixon was ranting on about it. He told Kissinger, his loyal servant, to relay orders to the Pentagon about the bombing of Cambodia. Kissinger immediately did so. His words to the military were: "Anything that flies on anything that moves." If you look through the archival record of all statistics, it would be hard to find a call for genocide that's so clear and explicit. And it wasn't just words, because it happened.

A few years ago, two leading Cambodia scholars, Taylor Owen and Ben Kiernan, published an article in Canada in which they discussed documents that had been released during the Clinton years about the bombing of Cambodia, and it turns out that it was known that the bombing was five times what had been reported. In fact, the bombing of rural Cambodia was greater than the total allied bombing in all theaters during World War II. And, as they point out, the effect of the bombing was to turn the Khmer Rouge from a marginal guerrilla group into a mass army of what they called enraged peasants who wanted to take revenge for this monstrous atrocity.

Well, we know what happened later. Did intellectuals react to this? It's easy to check. The Kiernan and Owen article, as far as I'm aware, appeared once in the US (on ZNet). I've never seen any other mention of it. It never received any comment that I've seen. The Kissinger remark disappeared. There was no comment on it when it was published. In fact, it was seen as a kind of a side remark in the article while the gossip was considered far more interesting. If you check the record, you'll find the same.

I've brought all this up repeatedly in talks in places like the Royal Institute of Philosophy in England, which is deeply concerned with issues of moral philosophy, as well as in the US to specialists on Cambodia and to journals that posture heroically about the terrible crimes of the Khmer Rouge. It's as if you're talking through a filter that cuts out certain words and phrases.

The Kissinger remark happened to be precisely at the time when the International Tribunal was trying Milošević. He died before the judgment. They were having a pretty hard time making a case. Suppose they had found a statement from Milošević saying, "Anything that flies on anything that moves." There would have been euphoria all over the Western world. He'd immediately have been tried and executed and we'd talk about how noble we are and so on. This is virtually 100 percent of intellectuals that I'm talking about.

**So we have a fact to explain: There are a finite number of people who fulfill the responsibility of intellectuals. They use their credibility and access to try and discuss reality in a way that is consistent with human well-being. Then we have virtually everyone else who has those advantages and who are incapable of even hearing the words to this background of interests. Why would so many people have the mental capacity to see the truth and not see the truth?**

Actually, Orwell had a word for it. He called it "doublethink"—the capacity to keep two contradictory ideas in mind and believe them both—practically a defining characteristic of intellectual history. I'm not talking just about the US. As far as I know, this is universal. I find very few exceptions. Furthermore, it goes back to early recorded history and every person who asks this question knows the answer. All they have to do is look at themselves. How many people have failed to go through an experience like, for example, when you're six years old, your little brother takes a toy, and you want the toy. Your mother's not looking, and you're bigger than he is, so you grab the toy. Your brother starts yelling, and your mother comes in and starts censuring you for taking the toy, and you say, "Yes, I took it because I wanted it and he's smaller than me." Or you say, "Look, he didn't want the toy anyway, and besides it was mine and he really stole it from me, so I was right." Do you know anyone who hasn't gone through that experience? We all know the answer to the question. There are easy ways to rationalize whatever happens in a complicated world in order to protect yourself.

The fact that intellectuals act like this is close to tautology. You don't become a respected intellectual unless you do this kind of thing—not like Kissinger's servility to the master—because you internalize it.

Take a look at history. There are people who don't do it—a small portion. Are they praised? Are they honored? They're usually treated very badly. It depends on the nature of the society. They can be thrown out of their jobs. In a civilized society like ours, they just get vilified and defamed. In a US possession like, say, El Salvador, they get their brains blown out and nobody there even cares about it or knows about it. In the post-Stalin Soviet Union, they get sent to prison or exiled.

We've just gone through a very revealing incident and how intellectuals reacted to it. In November 2009, there was an enormous celebration of some very critical events that took place in November 1989 when the Berlin Wall fell. Quickly, the Soviet Union collapsed. That was a major event in world history. There was a huge commemoration of it on the twentieth anniversary. What's written about it is mostly accurate but very revealing. It was heralded as a triumph of love and nonviolence, which overcame the Soviet Union. And that's the lesson we learned.

In fact, there's a generation of people who call themselves the "niners," as their consciousness was formed in November 1989 and they're dedicated to love and nonviolence. And that's what we learned in November 1989 when the Soviet Union collapsed.

Well, one week after the fall of the Berlin Wall something else happened. An elite Salvadoran Battalion had just come from several months of training at the JFK Special Forces School in Fort Bragg. This was the top battalion in the Salvadoran army, the pride of the US-run army. They broke into the university and murdered six leading Salvadoran intellectuals, Jesuit priests, and also their housekeeper and her daughter. In November 2009, the report was published in the Spanish press and was easily accessible. It presented the actual documents that ordered the assassination, signed by the chief of staff and top officials in the Salvadoran army, all so close to the Pentagon and the US embassy that you can barely find a ray of light between them—as had been suspected earlier but not proven. It was never published here or in England. So all that happened in 1989.

The killing of the Jesuit intellectuals closed off a decade of monstrous atrocities in El Salvador—maybe seventy thousand people killed, another one hundred thousand in Guatemala, who knows how many in Nicaragua—all organized by Washington in a massive terrorist war. In fact, the decade started with the assassination of the archbishop while he was reading Mass—done by the same hands.

So there's a huge event that took place that had to do with the history of the Catholic Church. The church of the early centuries was radically pacifist. That's why Christians were persecuted in the fourth century. The radical pacifist church was changed by the emperor Constantine, who took over and turned it into the church of the Roman Empire. The cross, which had been a symbol of the suffering of the poor, was now on the shield of the Roman Empire. From the fourth century almost to today, the church was the church of the rich and the persecutors.

In 1962, Pope John XXIII changed it. He called it Vatican II. At a big conference, they adopted the preferential option for the poor from the Gospels. That led, particularly in Latin America, to priests, nuns, and laypeople bringing the message of the gospel to poor peasants, trying to get them to think about their horrid conditions under US-dominated tyrannies and to try to organize and do something about it. Well, the US didn't wait long. It reacted immediately.

JFK organized a military coup in Brazil, one of the main centers. That established the first of the neo-Nazi-style national security states in Latin America—tortures, massacres, and so on. Brazil's a big country, so the dominoes started to fall, and country after country fell under a plague of repression that had no parallel since the conquistadors—Uruguay, Chile, Argentina—the latter probably the worst killers and President Reagan's favorites. It finally spread to Central America in the 1980s. Then came the hideous terrorist wars there. Throughout, a large part of it was a war against the church. We know who was responsible—the School of the Americas, which trained killers because they took pride in it. Take a look at the talking points in its advertisements. They take credit for the fact that, as it says, the US Army helped defeat liberation theology and the Church of the Gospel. That's a rather significant event. And it was effectively terminated in November 1989—not totally, there were residues—you can't kill ideas. Take a look and see how much commentary there was on it.

**Next to zero?**
I know of no comment here in Boston at Boston College, a Jesuit university, where I was one of the speakers. Another one of the speakers was Sabrino, one of the surviving Jesuit priests. He pointed out that the murdering of the Jesuit intellectuals was terrible enough, but much worse was murdering their housekeeper and her daughter who, as he put it, were symbols of the crucified population of US domains. How many comments were there on that? Actually, there was one comment. The hero of Eastern Europe, Vaclav Havel, came to the US shortly after the murder of his Jesuit colleagues in El Salvador. He gave a speech to a joint session of the US Congress and got a rousing ovation for calling the US the defenders

of freedom. The press and commentaries were euphoric, including some of the Left. The *Washington Post* had editorials asking why we can't have amazing intellectuals like this who tell us that we're the defenders of freedom after we slaughtered his counterparts in El Salvador—not to mention what came after. Does any of this enter history? Can it even be comprehended? I've talked about it. I get either a blank wall or else fury. Usually fury—"You're justifying Stalin."

**So in the case of incredible barbarism over extended periods of time, individuals who are considered intellectuals because they have accrued respect have almost reflexively followed the party line. Are there differences in their value systems or in their personalities that explain why they are over here and others are over there?**

The reasons vary. What's of general interest is how the system works. Suppose a kid in the third grade decides that what the teacher is saying is ridiculous and she's not going to do it. What usually happens is she becomes a behavior problem. If someone sitting next to her says, "Of course it's ridiculous, but I'm going to do it," so she goes on. There's a filtering system like this all the way from childhood.

If you're on a university faculty, you get letters of recommendation for students who want to apply or from faculty members looking for a job. There's some standard terminology that you get used to—"great, brilliant, wonderful, but lacks collegiality" or "is hard to get along with." What that usually means is she's a political radical or something like that. Nobody much will tell you, but it's kind of understood. And it's even understandable. You want your department to be collegial. You want people to be nice to each other. You don't want someone in your department getting up and saying, "Look, you're a war criminal," and demonstrating it.

You've had a little experience with this yourself. There are techniques that start from childhood, a massive filtering system. It's not 100 percent, even in totalitarian states, but they're very effective filtering systems that lead to certain outcomes. It's quite interesting to me and Ed Herman, and people who analyze the press. Journalists and commentators may say, "No one can tell me what to write." True, but if they didn't already know what to write, they wouldn't be there.

**So the solution, whether we're talking intellectuals or journalists, is in the structure of the situations they find themselves in as they produce**

**this kind of reflexive behavior to the point where they don't think about it. They don't say, "Okay, today I will lie about barbarism in order to get an extra star on my resume." They just do it.**

What you find, with very rare exceptions, is that it's pretty much the same thing in all disciplines. For instance, there's a huge study of foreign policy and international relations. I just happened to be reading one of the most prestigious international relations journals. One of the main themes in international relations is the impact of Wilsonian idealism. The study keeps entirely to words. So it says, "When Wilson mentioned self-determination, did he mean this or did he mean that?" And then there will be a big scholarly discussion of it.

Then you look at the letters he wrote to his wife, but you don't look at the facts. And the facts are glaringly obvious. Right now, for example, Haiti has been hit by an incredible disaster—hundreds of thousands of people killed, billions of dollars of damage. Everybody wants to give ten dollars to show how wonderful we are. Does Wilsonian idealism have anything to do with this? You'd have to be blind not to see it. Wilson was plenty of things, but he was one of the worst killers in Haiti. He destroyed the country, which was already pretty much destroyed by the French. He sent the Marines to Haiti on ridiculous pretexts. They killed thousands of people, according to Haitian historians, maybe fifteen thousand, and they reinstated virtual slavery.

Remember, Haiti was liberated by a slave revolt. One of the main things the US did was send the Marines to Haiti to disband Parliament at gunpoint. And the reason was very simple: The US had written a constitution. Actually, FDR took credit for it, probably boasting. Anyway, there was a written constitution which the Haitian Parliament refused to accept. Why? Because the constitution contained what were called in the US progressive measures, meaning permitting US corporations to buy up Haiti's land.

It's explained by economists and other "serious thinkers" that this was very progressive because obviously Haiti needed foreign investment. And how can you expect Americans to invest unless they own the place, so this was for the "benefit of Haitians" that we're doing this. If you read the press and commentary, we're just so benevolent; tears come to our eyes as we try desperately to help them.

At one point, the Marines ran a referendum in which 5 percent of the population participated. The traditional collaborating rich elite that you find in every colony voted something like a 99.9 percent approval. So it was a "democratic" election, and they got the progressive legislation with the obvious consequences. One of these was to add a further blow to the agricultural system, leading to urbanization for reasons that every economist will explain as very rational. That is, Haiti shouldn't produce rice. It's more efficient if highly subsidized US agribusiness floods Haiti with rice. Local rice farmers can't compete, so they are forced into the cities, where the women sew baseballs in miserable conditions in assembly plants. That's considered efficient.

So we drive them into the cities and destroy their agricultural system. Along comes a hurricane, a class-based disaster like most disasters. You take a look at the rich people's houses up in the hills. They get shaken up, but nothing much happens to them. Yet it's a huge catastrophe for the poor people living in the slums. Why are they there? Wilsonian idealism has a lot to do with it.

All of these things are happening at the same moment that scholarly articles are appearing about Wilsonian idealism and what he wrote to his wife and did he mean this, that, or the other thing. At the same moment, the front pages are showing us all about this hideous (class-based) disaster, which substantially results from one of many of Wilson's horrendous crimes.

Now we get back to Orwell and doublethink. If you want to be a respected intellectual, you have both of these ideas in your head at the same time. You believe both of them and don't notice the contradictions. This is overwhelming.

**Most of the time, there's this idea of objectivity. I'm wondering, as a precursor to that discussion, how bad journalism works and what the linchpins are and what is good journalism? What is it about the behavior of the *New York Times* that is so abhorrent, and what within the structure of the *NYT* causes it?**
First of all, the *NYT* is not very much different from the elite intellectual culture in general. My own view is that it's much more striking in scholarship. But in the *NYT* there are obvious institutional factors. The *NYT* is a major corporation—a huge corporate system. Like other businesses, it sells product to a market. The product is other businesses—advertisers—that's what keeps it going. The product for the *NYT* happens to be a fairly privileged audience. It's sometimes called the political class—the

20 percent of the population who are economic, political, and doctrinal managers. Furthermore, it is tightly linked to other institutions of power like the state, which is enormously under corporate influence.

**So you're saying that they're selling the 20 percent to companies; they're selling audience to advertisers. That's the real product they're selling.**
Right. They're also linked to state power, to other corporate power. These are the circles in which they live. That's who they have dinner with. There's a flow up and back. There's a small, elite group that has institutional roots and honest journalists who often do good work, but they do it within this framework. If they drift from the framework, they're usually cut off. Some quit in disgust.

It's kind of like the rest of the filtering system. So what do you expect to come out of this system? Suppose you're looking at it from Mars. You see huge corporations selling to privileged people—who are managers themselves—to other businesses, linked to the systems of power like the state, which are heavily influenced, in fact dominated, by these power systems.

**So what about good journalism?**
There are concrete examples. A couple of months ago, I happened to go to Mexico. I was invited to the twenty-fifth anniversary of a newspaper which, as far as I'm aware, is the only independent newspaper in the hemisphere. It's called *La Jornada*. It's very successful. It's the second-largest newspaper in Mexico, and it gets no commercial advertising because business hates it. It has very smart reporters who write for it and do investigative reporting. It has regional subsidiaries—I think it's the only Mexican newspaper that reports from Chiapas. How does it survive? They have a loyal subscriber base. I've learned a lot of important things from it that haven't appeared in the Western press.

**Are they "objective"?**
The notion of objectivity belongs in graduate school philosophy seminars. It doesn't apply in the real world. This is a topic for elite intellectuals to have abstract discussions about. Anybody, whoever they are, has a point of view. If you're doing quantum physics, you're looking at certain things and not at certain other things. Maybe what you're not looking at turns out to be extremely important. But you can't help having a point of view.

**So the whole discussion of objectivity is a waste of time?**
The discussion is a waste of time. There are places where you can see that the search for what is called balance is a charade. Take something like the survival of the species. There are two views on the matter of whether the species can have decent survival. One of them is 99.9 percent of scientists who say we are really getting into trouble with anthropogenic warming of the atmosphere. On the other side, there's Rush Limbaugh, Glenn Beck, Sara Palin, Congressperson Inhofe. An article anywhere in the *Times* has to have "balance" so you get those positions and, of course, there's a ton of advertising from the business world that wants you to believe it's not happening, which is kind of interesting because the executives who are doing this advertising know exactly as well as the scientists that it is happening and they know it's going to destroy their grandchildren and everything they own, but they still want people not to believe it.

There are institutional factors there too. They go back to the nature of markets in which the future of the species is an externality. You don't consider it when you are involved in transactions. Anyway, it's happening, and we see the results, which have been so incredible that by now there's a sharp decline in the US in the belief in anthropogenic global warming. That's a death sentence for the species—I'm really not exaggerating—we can argue about the time span.

You see it if you're in a market system. Take these executives. Say you're the CEO of ExxonMobil. You read everything. You know what's happening, you know that the danger is extremely severe and that the longer we wait, the worse it's going to be, but that's what economists call an externality. It doesn't enter into your day-to-day decisions.

In your day-to-day decisions in a market system, you are forced to look at certain things and not others. You are forced to look at short-term profit and market share. If you don't do that, you're out of a job. You can rationalize doing it on grounds of "If I didn't do it, I'd be out and then I couldn't do good things for anybody." That's the grounds on which it's done. Not that "I'll be out," but that "I'm doing the right thing for the world because, if I get people not to believe in what I know is true, then maybe they'll put more money into solar energy and maybe I'll make some profit out of that"—as they are now trying to do. In the long run, they say, it's good for the species.

**One of the dynamics you mention is that if you're an intellectual or a journalist, there's a price to pay for being good. We can't affect that**

**entirely, but can you name some journalists around the world and in the US who deserve to be known? It would be helpful if those considering journalism school had models.**

Correspondents on the ground do extremely good work. If I was on a desert island somewhere and I was allowed to have only one newspaper, I'd get the *NYT*. It gives you tolerable pictures of what's going on in the world, and the correspondents on the ground typically don't lie. They describe accurately what they see. Same with the AP wires.

It's kind of interesting that the book Edward Herman and I wrote, *Manufacturing Consent*, is hated by journalists, the press, and intellectuals because they claim the book attacked the press. It's unfair because a large part of the book is defending the press against attacks from what are considered the liberals—Freedom House—the main institution that's supposed to support freedom and democracy.

They launched a huge attack on the press with several volumes of denunciations claiming that the press lost the war in Vietnam because they "lied" about the Tet Offensive and they were pro-Communist, and so antagonistic to the US that they distorted what happened and therefore we lost this "noble war."

Ed and I went through the two Freedom House volumes. We found a phenomenal number of outright lies. When we looked at the facts, what we found was that the reporters on the ground were reporting what happened honestly, courageously, and accurately, and within a framework that is destroyed by ideological fanaticism.

So somebody would write an article saying that the Air Force came and bombed a place to smithereens and the soldiers came in and killed everybody that was around and that it's necessary to defend democracy and freedom in South Vietnam. So the reporters were accurate but deeply ideological. In contrast, the Freedom House was just lying through their teeth.

**Then, presumably, the model of a good reporter, journalist, and commentator is somebody who not only relays the facts that they see, but who is not subject to that narrow ideological frame.**

Let me give an example from the period when the My Lai massacre took place, 1968. The news of the massacre finally broke through, thanks to Sy Hersh, an independent journalist working for Dispatch News Service. He was a very smart guy. He picked the moment of a huge demonstration in

Washington—a million people, lots of journalists—to release the information on My Lai publicly. Actually, it had been around for a year and a half, but nobody had paid attention to it. So Sy Hersh released it, and it became a big thing—kind of a symbol for everything that went wrong. It's a wonderful symbol for liberal intellectuals because they can blame it on half-crazed GIs in the field who didn't know who was going to shoot at them next.

There were a couple of journalists, namely Kevin Buckley, who was the Saigon correspondent for *Newsweek*. He and an associate did a detailed analysis of the context of My Lai. This was part of what was called the post-Tet pacification campaigns—a huge mass murder operation to which My Lai was a minuscule footnote. It was such a small footnote that the Quaker Hospital, which was near where My Lai took place, never bothered mentioning it because similar events were happening all over the place.

Buckley wrote this all up, and *Newsweek* wouldn't publish it. He gave it to Ed Herman and me, and we wrote about it in *The Political Economy of Human Rights*, published in 1979 by South End Press. What we pointed out was that, yes, it took place, and it's easy to focus on it because you can blame it on bad guys. But what was actually taking place in air-conditioned rooms where people just like us were sitting was incomparably more horrendous. Do you think anybody ever mentioned that?

But what Kevin Buckley and his associate did was really good journalism.

# Science, Religion, and Human Nature

**ALBERT:** What's rationality and irrationality?

**CHOMSKY:** An example of extreme irrationality is what we've just been talking about. Orwell called it "doublethink," the ability to have two contradictory ideas in your mind at the same time and to believe both of them. That's the peak of irrationality and that virtually defines the elite intellectual community.

Now let's take concrete examples of fundamentalist irrationality. In January 2002, before the invasion of Iraq, George Bush was trying to get international support for the invasion, and he met with French president Chirac. In this meeting, Bush started ranting about a very obscure passage from the book of Ezekiel that nobody understands. It's a passage about Gog and Magog, and nobody knows if they're people or places or whatever. But Gog and Magog are supposed to come from the North to attack Israel, and then we get into ultrafanatic Christian Evangelical madness.

Bush told the story of how Gog and Magog attacked Israel and there was Armageddon. Everybody gets slaughtered, and the souls who are saved rise to heaven. Reagan apparently believed it too. When his handlers couldn't control him and he was off by himself, he'd start raving about this stuff. For Reagan, Gog and Magog were Russia, for Bush they were Iraq. Bush told all this to Chirac, who didn't have a clue what Bush was talking about, so he approached the French Foreign Office and asked, "Do you know what this man is raving about?" They didn't know either. So Chirac approached a pretty well-known Belgian theologian who wrote sort of a disquisition on this passage about the way it's interpreted and what it might mean.

How do I know about this? I know because the Belgian theologian sent me a copy of it with background on the story. I never published it because it sounded so off-the-wall. Finally, I was talking to an Australian academic and researcher and mentioned it to him, and he decided to look into it. It turns out to be correct. In fact, the story appears in Chirac's biography, so the incident actually happened.

So here's the world in the hands of a raving lunatic who is talking about Gog and Magog and Armageddon and souls rising to heaven—and the world survived.

## Science

**Okay, what's science? Why is something scientific. What marks something as being sensible science or nonsensical nonscience masquerading as science? And how do you feel about left critics of science who say it's imperial and sexist or rooted in Western whatever?**
There's a category of intellectuals who are undoubtedly pretty sincere. If you look at it from the outside, what they're actually doing is using polysyllabic words and complicated constructions, which they seem to understand because they talk to each other. Most of the time I can't understand what they're talking about, and they're supposed to be in my field. It's all very inflated. It has a terrible effect on the Third World. In the First World, with the richest countries, it doesn't really matter as much if a lot of nonsense goes on in the Paris cafés or the Yale comparative literature department. On the one hand, the popular movements in the Third World, etc. need serious intellectuals to participate. If they're all ranting postmodern absurdities, well, they're gone. I've seen examples. So there is that category of intellectuals, and it's considered left-wing and very advanced.

Some of what appears in it makes sense, but when you reproduce it in monosyllables, it turns out to be truisms. So, yes, it's perfectly true that if you look at scientists in the West, they're mostly men. It's perfectly true that women have had a hard time breaking into the scientific fields and it's perfectly true that there are institutional factors determining how science proceeds that reflect power structures. All of this can be described in monosyllables. On the other hand, you don't get to be a respected intellectual by presenting truisms in monosyllables.

So when so-called left criticism happens to be accurate, that's fine, but a lot of left criticism seems to be pure nonsense. In fact, that's been demonstrated conclusively. There's an important book that goes through the most respected French intellectuals and run through what they say about science, and it's so embarrassing that you cringe when you read it. One of the most striking is from Latour, who has a background in science. Latour wrote an article ridiculing an article in which the author claimed that one of the Pharaohs had died of tuberculosis. Latour says it's totally absurd because TB had only been discovered in the nineteenth century and, because everything's a social construction, it never happened. Kind of on the level of Bush and Gog/Magog. This is all taken very seriously and considered very left.

**But one point to look at, I think, is that the description of intellectuals, journalists, and this part of what calls itself the Left, shows there is something similar going on. You have those guys sitting in the air-conditioned rooms bombing the hell out of the world for their careers and their status because of the reflexive lessons they learned. Then you have those who are in literary criticism, or whatever field they might be in, who are obscuring or dressing it up for similar reasons.**

If you look at what's happened, it's pretty easy to figure out. Suppose you're a literary scholar at some elite university or an anthropologist or whatever. If you do your work seriously, that's fine, but you don't get any prizes for it. On the other hand, take a look at the rest of the universe. They've got these guys in the physics department and the math department and they have all kinds of complicated theories, which we can't understand, but they seem to understand them. And they have principles, and they do experiments, and they find either they work or they don't work, and that seems like really impressive stuff. Since they want to be like that too, they want to have a theory too. We're just like the physicists. They talk incomprehensibly; we can talk incomprehensibly. They have big words; we'll have big words. They draw far-reaching conclusions; we'll have far-reaching conclusions. We're just as prestigious as they are, and that's appealing.

There are other things that went on. Remember, a lot of this stuff comes from Paris. Interesting things were happening in Paris in the 1970s. French intellectuals were the last group of intellectuals in the world who were overwhelmingly dedicated Stalinists and Maoists. It was very standard and respected. By the mid-1970s that was getting to be a pretty hard position to uphold. If you take a look at what happened, there was a sudden shift. People who had been flaming Maoists and Stalinists suddenly became the first people in the world to have discovered the Gulag and went on a tear about how everyone else supported Stalinist/Maoist atrocities—and we're French so we have to be in front of everyone else, so we exposed it. Now we're open to the new philosophy.

One of the leading French cultural theorists, who happened to visit me around 1974, was a flaming Maoist. A couple of years later she was one of the first people to have "discovered" Stalinist/Maoist atrocities. When you go through that transition, you've got to do something else or how are you going to be on the front pages? Okay, along comes the invention of poststructuralism.

## Religion
**Let's move on. What do you think of religion?**
It depends on what you mean by religion. Do you mean the Abrahamic religions—Judaism, Christianity, and Islam? Buddhism is different, spiritual beliefs among Native Americans are different, Hindus are different.

**But what is religion, per se?**
A belief that there is something in the world that is beyond our grasp which is determining the way things happen, and it will be a consolation to people because they'll see their loved ones who have died, and there's a spiritual force beyond our grasp is probably ubiquitous and understandable. The sun is going around the earth, we can see it, so something must be happening like Apollo on his chariot pulling the sun. Or why is my child dying? He didn't do anything. So there's got to be some explanation.

**So it's a set of stories to make sense of reality, but it's not science?**
Well, Apollo pulling the chariot is kind of early science. It's a theory; it's worked out, not trivial. The classical Greeks discovered a lot of things.

**But now, when there's lots of evidence other than that, it's no longer science?**
That just means our understanding has deepened. The transition from magic to science is a pretty smooth transition. Even the word "science" in English didn't appear until the mid-nineteenth century. There was a word, but it meant something else. In the mid-nineteenth century, there was a divorce between science and philosophy. Before it was just philosophy. In fact, if you go to Oxford, let's say, you can study natural philosophy and

moral philosophy. Natural philosophy is what we in the US call natural sciences. Moral philosophy is what we call the humanities. So the whole concept of science is a pretty recent one. And there was an intellectual revolution. It began with Galileo and it went on and led to enormous insights and after a while science took off and became a special domain.

In the early nineteenth century, Kant couldn't have told you whether he was a philosopher or a scientist. He taught astronomy and moral philosophy. An intelligent, educated person did all those things. By the mid-nineteenth century, it became very hard to do all those things. The sciences were reaching a point where we began to understand this and you couldn't be a person who knows everything. So things got professionalized and what we call science became a separate domain. Recall how recent this is. Prior to that, people were trying to figure things out and we might call what they were trying to figure out magic. These were pretty smart people.

Take, say, Isaac Newton. People laugh about the fact that he spent most of his life on chemistry and Church fathers. There was alchemy in Church fathers. In terms of what was called Corpustian theories, everybody accepted that the world was made up of little building blocks like bricks. Shift a few years and you get gold from lead.

As for the Church fathers, that made perfect sense too. Newton was coming right after the humanist period when they had discovered the wealth and richness of classical civilizations, which hadn't been known. The belief expanded that these guys really understood something and they were kind of keeping it a secret, doing it in esoteric ways. If we didn't decode what they were doing, we'd get off on wonderful discoveries. So it wasn't an irrational pursuit.

## Sectarianism

**I want to switch to a political variant of the things we've been talking about, which is the term "sectarianism."**
Sometimes it's genuine disagreements, which should be worked out with solidarity and mutual sympathy and support. We've all been in activist groups—long meetings, real issues to discuss. So that's the right kind of sectarianism. Then there's a lot of ego-tripping: "I want to be Lenin, so follow me. I've got my doctrines and my ideology, and if you can't accept them, you're an enemy of the working people"—whatever it happened to be. It's extremely common among groups that don't have much mass support, that are kind of isolated, that either don't have a lot to do or

believe they don't have a lot to do, and sectarianism is one way of avoiding engagement. It's rampant and it's pretty ugly.

**But it's not only the behavior that's holding viewpoints in a sectarian fashion, it's holding views in a fundamentalist fashion that has the element of "it's true because it's doctrine; it's true because it's in a book; it's true because I believe it or someone I admire believes it." And it's unchangeable.**

That kind of sectarianism can destroy groups. In fact, any decent government infiltrator—and there are plenty of them—would want to simulate that kind of sectarianism. In the 1960s, one of the things every group had to learn the hard way was that even in your small circle there's a provocateur. After a while, it was possible to pick them out. They were the ones who were going to show up at the trials and that sort of thing. Sometimes it doesn't need to be a provocateur. A lot of these small groups are parasitic and try to recruit, so they join, they work, they sit in meetings longer than anyone, and they try to get some kind of position of control and then recruit people to their particular sect.

**But I'm also talking about good people who have been in their lives perfectly sensible, who then, for whatever reason, adopt a set of views and are no longer open to the possibility that those views could be wrong. They no longer see the world except in terms of those views. They're not police. What's the antidote to the phenomenon?**

That's part of life. Take, say, Einstein. He just wouldn't believe that God could play dice. For an individual, try to be as open and sympathetic to others as you can. It's not easy in complicated situations, even in the hard sciences. I find it all the time in professional work.

In general, there isn't a structural antidote. I don't criticize Einstein for not wanting to believe quantum theoretical approaches. In fact, a lot of good experiments came out of them. That's the way humans ought to be, as long as it doesn't get to the point where it becomes a personal ego trip or an effort to take over and control. These are aspects of human life that you have to deal with.

## Creationism

**There is the creationism phenomenon that bears on science also. What's your reaction?**

24

First of all, it comes from a religious course. A lot of it is genuine. People do not want to accept the idea that what they interpret as meaning is determined. Science doesn't mean that, but if you have a superficial understanding of science—in fact, if you read what plenty of scientists and philosophers say, it's basically, "Look, you don't have any free will. You don't have any choices. Everything's determined. You're just acting out in a system of controls."

I don't want to believe that and, in fact, I don't. So I can easily see why other people don't want to believe it. Rather, they want to believe that there's something going on in the world. Maybe they can't grasp it, but there's a force somewhere that is trying to make us better, make the world better, make good things happen, enable me to see my child in heaven. One consequence of this array of beliefs is the belief that the world was created. The founding fathers were mostly called deists. The idea was that God was a retired engineer. He got the whole thing started, gave it a kick in the pants, then left, and we're supposed to run it. That was kind of the secular religion that was common at the time.

At the same time, the US, since its origins, has been off the spectrum in extremist religious beliefs—belief in miracles and the devil and that the world was created seven thousand years ago, and so on. To some extent, you find it in industrial societies. You find it in England, but the US is literally off the graph. The country was founded by religious extremists. Remember the settlers of New England were following God's will. There's a streak in US history called Providentialism. It goes all the way from the founding fathers, so-called, to current presidents. "God has a conception of history and we're acting it out." The way this was applied is pretty remarkable. So, for example, the English settlers in New England—the *Mayflower*. The first Charter of the Massachusetts Bay Colony given by King Charles in 1628 and the goal of the Massachusetts Colony was to bring the benefits of civilization to the Indians who were "pleading for it."

If you look at the great seal of the Massachusetts Bay Colony, around 1629, it's very revealing. It ought to be on the wall of every classroom in the country. It's the founding of the country. It shows an Indian with spears pointed down as a sign of peace. Out of the Indian's mouth is a scroll that says "Come over and help us." The colonists were carrying out what is now called the responsibility to protect, a fancy term for imperialism. So they were coming over to answer the plea of the indigenous population. That's when the famous phrase "city on a hill" was produced. In 1630,

John Winthrop gave a famous statement and said we're like a city on the hill; we're not like any other country in the world—benevolent, selfless, coming over to answer pleas of the Indians. That goes right to today. That's a leading theme of scholarship, that we're different from everyone else because we're a city on a hill—"a shining city on a hill," as Reagan put it. It goes right to this minute, and the reason comes from our answering the plea of the natives to help them. That was explained too. Take a look at a leading Supreme Court justice's comments. He says, "Well, you know, the ways of God are mysterious. Although we came to help the Indians, we tried. Everything we did was in their interest, but somehow they withered away"—that's the phrase they used. Like the leaves in autumn, they just kind of blew away.

In the early twentieth century, it was pretty hard to go on with this, so you have people like Theodore Roosevelt, one of the most extreme racist murderers in American history—that's why he's on Mount Rushmore, who during the second term of his presidency, around 1906, gave a talk to a group of missionaries in which he explained to them that it was to the benefit of the native population that we exterminated them because it enabled a superior race to replace them. That was very common. You can read things like that in Walt Whitman or Ralph Waldo Emerson.

This is an extremely racist country, and they invented a mythology of Anglo-Saxonism [saying that] we're all Anglo-Saxons. Jefferson, for example, who was a big believer in this, said that we've got to go back to the eighth century when there were pure Anglo-Saxons, before they were contaminated by others and that's the ideal of humanity, justice, and everything else. Benjamin Franklin, for example, thought we shouldn't allow immigration of Germans and Swedes because they're not white enough. They're a little off color. But we, the Anglo Saxons, carry civilization forward. It's incredible, the history of it all. Hitler looks mild in comparison. This goes right through American history. Wilsonian idealism is part of American exceptionalism. One aspect of these beliefs is what most of the world would call religious extremism, which includes what was called "great reawakenings," periods of mass enthusiasm because Christ was coming or whatever it may be. It changed in the last years in an interesting way. Although it had been right through American history, it never entered the core political system, but it influenced things.

I don't think it's ever been studied, but I think it came from Jimmy Carter, an honest, sincere, fundamentalist Christian. He probably believed everything he was saying. Most of what the world sees as off-the-wall, he believed. I think the party managers—American elections are basically run by the public relations industry—recognized that if you pretend to be a devout Christian, you pick up 30 percent of the vote. In fact, every presidential candidate since Carter has professed to be a devout Christian. Take, say, Bill Clinton. He's about as religious as I am. His handlers made sure that every Monday morning there was a photograph of him at church singing hymns. It's appealing to things that are deep in American culture and it's intertwined with racism, with Anglo-Saxon fanaticism, with "come and help us."

**You've been skeptical of what are called conspiracy theories—from the Kennedy assassination through 9-11. What advice would you give to people who are trying to figure out when elites are conspiring and when they are doing business as usual?**
Take World War II. We're not talking about the Roosevelt administration—the most liberal administration ever. From 1939 to '45, there were regular meetings taking place of high-level State Department planners. The Council on Foreign Relations, which is the out-of-government organization of businesspeople and others who had an interest in foreign policy. It wasn't a secret organization, but there were a lot of conspiracy theories about it. They had something called a war and peace studies group in which they were planning for the postwar world.

**Why's that a conspiracy?**
They were conspiring about what to do in the postwar world. They laid out principles that are still being carried out. Their principles are almost the same as those the government developed in the late 1940s. That's a conspiracy, and there's only one book about it, *Imperial Brain Trust* by Laurence Shoup and William Minter. It was an open conspiracy that people on the left barely mention. It had a lot of consequences. In the 1940s, General Motors, Firestone, and Standard Oil of California conspired to buy up and destroy the very efficient electric railway system in Los Angeles and many other places and convert it to fossil fuels—trucks, cars, and so on.

That was one part of a huge social engineering project involving the government, corporations, and others, which changed the country into something that may now destroy the species with the wasteful use of fossil fuels. They were taken to court and sentenced. They got a fine—$5,000 or something like that. That was a conspiracy with tremendous consequences and there have been many more like it.

**Is there a difference between that and the Kennedy assassination theories?**
One difference is that these are major conspiracies with huge consequences. But what people are looking for—like the people who listen to Rush Limbaugh—they want an answer. The world is rotten so there must be something going on that we don't know about. There's only one interesting question I know of about the Kennedy assassination: Was it a high-level conspiracy with policy consequences? If it wasn't, unless you worship royalty, then I don't see why it's any different from any other killing. I have friends who are concerned with something else. They want to show that it was a done at a high level, taking away from us this magnificent person who was going to do all sorts of terrific things and make it a better world, and it's because they killed him that we got into the awful mess we're in. Well, there are ways of investigating that. You can look at Kennedy's policies, statements, and actions. You can look at what followed when his advisors (same people, including the doves) made the decisions. You can see that Kennedy was to the hawkish side of his administration. He was dragged reluctantly into support for civil rights and a few other things. Meanwhile, he was carrying out terrorist wars against Cuba right to the day of the assassination. Furthermore, nothing changed. The ones who were advising him on withdrawal changed because the facts changed.

There isn't the slightest piece of evidence of a high-level conspiracy. So you look for something else. The CIA and others. There's a huge industry about that with factoids.

If you have no conception of what a theory and explanation is—and most people outside the sciences don't—what you do is collect factoids. This happens, that happens, how do you explain this? If you looked at science that way you would despise all of science. It has no significance, unless you believe in the Camelot story that Kennedy was about to do the most magnificent things and that's why he was killed. But then you had to have evidence for that. When you look at those stories, even those from really good historians, the kind of evidence they give is shocking.

The main idea is that Kennedy was kind of a Machiavellian; that he had these plans to do all kinds of things, but he had to conceal them from his advisors because they would have blocked them. He, therefore, said we can't get out of Vietnam before victory in order to delude Robert McNamara and others so they wouldn't really know that he was going to get out—and it goes on and on like this. It's all just worship of royalty. It's kind of nice to feel that something magnificent was happening, and the Camelot story is an easy one to believe in. And Kennedy was no fool. He understood right away that if you want to get good press and a good record, you butter up the intellectuals. Make them think you love them—and he did. In the early 1960s in Cambridge, every morning Harvard professors got on the Eastern shuttle flying down to Washington to have lunch with Jackie and say hello to Jack and talk to Dean and all that kind of stuff. Then they'd come back in the evening glowing with joy at how they were rubbing shoulders with royalty and so the Kennedys got very good images. But if you try to look at the facts, the Camelot story shrivels away.

The 9-11 conspiracy story is pretty interesting. A third to half the people at the center of it, as far as I can tell, are involved in political activism. Most of them are drawn into it and they have factoids too—like somebody found nanothermites, whatever the hell that is, in the bottom of building seven. That's the core of a large part of the evidence.

Some of the people writing this become experts in physics and civil engineering on the basis of an hour on the internet. They've managed to collect a small scattering of architects and one or two people who are supposed to be scientists and a couple of others who write articles for 9-11 studies and some online journal.

So that "proves" the scientific world is with them. Then comes the big story which ignores some obvious questions. If the Bush administration was responsible, why did they blame the Saudis? Were they insane? They wanted to invade Iraq so why blame the Saudis? If they had blamed the Iraqis, it's an open-and-shut case. The whole country is behind you, you get a UN resolution, NATO supports you, and you go ahead and invade Iraq. But they blamed the Saudis, so they had to jump through hoops. They tried to invent stories about weapons of mass destruction and blame al-Qaeda and eventually invaded Iraq. So are they lunatics? That's one possibility, of course. Is there another explanation for why they blamed the Saudis?

**Because it would have been too obvious to blame Iraq?**
That's exactly what you get from the conspiracy theorists. Huge efforts have gone into this for seven years. No one's ever been indicted and they were never going to be. It does have an effect—it diverts a lot of energy

and effort from trying to do something like stop the war in Iraq. That takes effort and is costly.

They also feel extremely brave because it feels so risky to write a note on the internet to say, "I think Bush is really a bad guy," and then they find stories about me and others who don't go along and we're considered CIA stooges or "left gatekeepers" that the government inserts into popular movements and who are trying to stop the real criticism—"like Bush put the bombs in Building Seven." So they build up stories and a lot of people believe them. It's a little like believing that the reason why my life is collapsing is because the rich liberals, who own the corporations, are giving everything away to illegal immigrants. People who are at a loss don't trust anything, and rightly. They don't trust institutions. They think they're lying to them, and nothing makes any sense. These things have a certain appeal—like Rush Limbaugh.

**When you think of it, it means that 30–40 percent of the US population believes that Bush carried out 9-11. There's virtually nothing the Left can say to that 30–40 percent that's worse than that. So you have to ask why that 30–40 percent isn't doing anything, given that they think they are run by a mass murderer who wants to kill all the people.**
I ask a lot of people about that. So you think you're being run by a maniac who wants to kill everybody. Why don't you do something about it? The answer is always the same thing: "It's hopeless, there's nothing we can do, and we're victims of some powerful force." It's easier to give up. That happens with a lot of things. Take, say, the Israeli lobby story. It's extremely convenient to believe that the Israeli lobby controls the US. The other thing is that it preserves American innocence. We are still the city on the hill, it's just that we're being led around by "these Jews." What can we do?

## Human Nature
**Which brings me to my next question: Is there such a thing as human nature? Or are the groups of people who deny the possibility of such a thing correct in doing so?**
Either there is such a thing as human nature or people are angels from another planet or another universe. Any organism that exists in the organic world has a nature. That's what distinguishes it from other organisms. So, we're different from insects, we're different from apes. That can either be that we're different from other organisms because we have some

kind of a nature or because maybe God planted us in the world. Those are the two options. Marxists, even well-known Marxists like Gramsci, say there's no human nature, there's just history. You can find a couple of phrases like that. They can't have meant what they said. What they probably meant was human nature can take many different forms. But this has become some kind of slogan. It's considered, on what's called the Left, that if you deny that there's any human nature, you're in favor of change. If you say there is no human nature, you are reactionary because you're saying people have to be rotten and have slaves. If you take a look at Marx, he was a dedicated believer in human nature. In fact, he took most of his ideas right out of the Enlightenment and the Romantic Period, and carried them over to his concept of alienation. Somehow your fundamental nature is in need of some kind of creative work under your own control. It's based on a concept of human nature.

Is there any evidence for it? Let's assume we're not angels, we're organisms; therefore, that is human nature. Okay, then we try to discover what it is. We do that in the same way we discover what bee nature is. It's much harder as we're much more complicated organisms and, unlike with other organisms, we can't conduct experiments. But if you want to study the parts of human nature that have to do with the issues that matter to human affairs, you can't do anything much in the way of comparative evidence because humans are different. What evidence there is is an evolutionary difference of twelve to fifteen million years. There are experimental issues in some areas. Take, say, language, where I work. There's quite a lot of evidence that it's a unique human property. There's nothing remotely like it in the animal world as far as I know, but you can learn a lot about it because you can separate it from other things. Actually, many of the questions you'd like to ask about language are beyond experiment and traditional questions like how you and I are doing what we're now doing. How are we able to produce new expressions, have new ideas—what's sometimes called the creative aspect of language use—which is a big topic in the tradition of Descartes, Rousseau, and others. But we can't study that. We can study the mechanisms that enter into it but not much else. As soon as you get to choice and decisions, you're kind of at sea. There are lots of topics we can study. There are many beyond what we know how to study, but there's got to be a nature. Otherwise, we're angels or like amoebas—anything that happens to us affects us and we become some shapeless form.

**Otherwise a human baby could grow to be a penguin.**

Exactly. There's a huge debate about whether there's an innate language faculty. The answer to that is so trivial you wonder who's asking the question. If my granddaughter and her pet chimp or songbird or whatever have exactly the same data, how come my granddaughter picks out the data that's language-related, reflexively, and ends up doing what you and I are doing, whereas the other animals don't even take the first step. Either it's a miracle or she's got a language facility, there's no other option. But there's a huge debate about that even among people called scientists. People are extremely irrational about themselves for some reason but, yes, there has to be a human nature and we can try to find out what it is. On issues that really matter to us, science doesn't tell us that much. They tell a little, for example, why are people altruistic? Why do they help others? There's some evidence from biology that some of it gives us a basis for what we know already.

People tend to be more caring for their children. You can then give a story about kin selection. The genes that get proliferated, it tells you something. It doesn't tell you why people go into icy waters to try and rescue stranded dolphins. It doesn't tell you why we do that, but don't care about a kid starving across the street, or why we take care of our stepchildren.

There's one category, reciprocal altruism, worked on by Robert Trevor, who's a good biologist. There are some interesting results—you help me, I help you. Mostly you have to rely on intuition, introspection, experience, examples from history, and you get some speculations of what humans are like.

**What's the utility of the view that there's no such thing as human nature?**

The utility is that you can convince yourself, if you are sufficiently irrational, that we can introduce changes. These features are useful for people who want to be managers. If there's no human nature, if we can control people, there's no moral barrier to it. We can determine what they can be, and we can be benevolent and help these amoebas turn into good things instead of bad things. It's a very convenient doctrine for the managerial class.

**There are people who will respond to the idea of justice, fairness, people controlling their own lives by saying it sounds nice, but human nature**

**precludes it and yields instead what we see all around us. How would you counter that widespread view?**
Two ways: First, the way you try to encounter any factual statement—back it up. Do you have a scientific basis for it? Do you have evidence for it?

**They're going to say that the evidence is all around us.**
So is evidence of benevolence and dedication to improving things. They're picking certain features from history which have an interesting consequence—that is, they prevent you from doing anything. It's very self-serving, if nothing can be changed. Then it's fine if you just want to be Ayn Rand or something. But you have no evidence for it. If you take a look at history, you're just as likely to find the opposite. You can show in history that Kropotkin was right in saying that mutual aid is a factor in evolution.

So you take the range of history and experience and you pick out something that will justify your looking out for number one, or you can take something that will justify you devoting yourself to the welfare of others. It's your choice, but you can't claim any argument from history. In fact, if you really take the argument from history seriously, there is something noticeable. There is a tendency towards more and more commitment to justice, equity, and freedom. You see it pretty clearly—even in our own lifetimes. Take women's rights, civil rights, concern over future generations—these were limited years ago.

**One of the interesting things to me is that when people engage in antisocial behavior, they have to act as if that's not what they're doing. They cover it with a rationalizations. Why would you need to do that? If antisocial behavior was wired in, we wouldn't have to alibi it. A wolf wouldn't say, "I'm eating the sheep because I'm trying to help the sheep." It would say, "I'm eating the sheep because I'm hungry." The same thing goes for humans.**
Henry Kissinger would probably say it about the Cambodian bombing, but that's a good argument. Why bother to rationalize?

# Education and Economics

**ALBERT:** What's the purpose of education in US society?

**CHOMSKY:** A lot of the purpose, which has always been there, is training for obedience and conformity. Actually that's been a substantial development since the 1960s movements in this direction. The 1960s were very frightening to elites—liberal, right-wing, whoever. They didn't like the fact that too many people were becoming too independent. The literature focused on the crazy fringe, of course, but what really worried them was not the crazy fringe but the mainstream, which was mobilizing the country and was raising questions that were difficult and unpleasant—war, sexism, all sorts of things—but the real problem is that people were becoming too independent. It was so overwhelming they couldn't keep quiet about it.

There's a very important book, which everyone should read—the first publication of the Trilateral Commission—the liberal international elite forum for the US, Europe, and Japan. They were worried about what they called "excessive democracy." Groups of people who were usually passive and apathetic were beginning to enter the political arena and press their own demands. They needed to damp it down and have more of what they called "moderation" in democracy. One of the things that concerned them was students. Part of the proposal, which came from Harvard professor Samuel Huntington, among others, was that there was a failure of the institutions that were responsible for the "indoctrination of the young." This phrase is usually kept under wraps, but it came out when there was enough concern. The institutions responsible for the indoctrination of the young—schools, universities, and churches—weren't doing their job, and "we had to do something about it."

This was part of a very widespread phenomenon; it runs over into the law and order efforts of Nixon. It includes the drug wars, which were motivated by this to a substantial extent, including the mythology that was concocted about the "addicted" army and all sorts of other things. It shows up in raising tuitions and other disciplinary techniques for the young to try and indoctrinate them. It continues right to the present. The Obama administration, for example, has stiffened and extended the Bush proposals of what's called No Child Left Behind, which came from the liberals. No Child Left Behind is a euphemism for "train to test." Don't allow children to be creative, make sure they pass that next test. And there's pressure because the teacher's salary depends on it—evaluations and so on.

Well, all of us, anyone who went to a good school, got there because we were obedient enough to do this idiotic stuff. So you have a test coming, you memorize what you have to memorize. Two days later you forget it. Then you go on and do what you feel like. Anyone who hasn't had this experience is pretty unusual. But now it's the framework for teaching, and I think it goes back to the concern about the failure of the institutions that indoctrinate the young. Let me give you a personal example: When I was in Mexico I gave some talks at UNAM—the major university, a couple of hundred thousand students, very high-quality, and a good campus. It's free. I also gave talks at a city university, which is not only free, but it's open. Anybody can go. A lot of people aren't ready to go—so there are preparatory courses—also quite high-quality. I was impressed. The city university was established by the leftist mayor—it's running, it's doing good things. That's Mexico, a poor country. From there, I happened to go to California for talks. California may be the richest place in the world. It had a great public education system, the best anywhere. It's being destroyed.

In the major universities—Berkeley and UCLA—tuitions are going up so high that it has become like a private university. Furthermore, they have big endowments, like private universities do, and likely will be privatized. So these jewels in the crown will become like Yale and Harvard.

The rest of the system meanwhile is being degraded. That's in one of the richest places. Mexico's one of the poorest places. It's not for economic reasons that Mexico has probably the only major independent newspaper in the hemisphere. These are social decisions.

The education system is being constructed consciously—you can read the legislation and commentary—essentially to indoctrinate. That's what training to test means. Teachers I have talked to—and students and parents—have told me about it. One parent told me about her daughter in the sixth grade who was interested in a topic that came up in class and asked her teacher if she could learn more about it. The teacher said, "Sorry, we can't talk about that because it doesn't come up on the test and we have to make sure that you pass the test." I'm sure that comes up all the time.

Okay, there are forms of indoctrination, imposing discipline, and so on. They've always been there. One of the impressive things about the US educational history, by comparative standards, is that the US set up a mass public education system way before Europe did. And the US had big research universities, which Europe didn't have. A lot of the economic success of the US is based on it. But even at the very beginning, a large part of the purpose of the US educational system was to turn independent farmers into disciplined factory workers, which was a big change and farmers didn't like it. There were a lot of battles and struggles about it. You go back to the nineteenth century, working people regarded wage labor as practically slavery. They had to drive that out of people's heads and get them to work in big economic institutions where they're essentially cogs in a machine.

**In this view, the current educational system, while there are holes, basically aims to make students capable of enduring boredom, obeying orders, and learning the skills that are called for by the system they're about to enter. That means there's a sector that's going to run the system that learns skills needed for elites, managers, etc. That's the picture of education as we know it. So what's good education?**

There are examples of it. Take where I am, at MIT. It's a science-based university, research-oriented. Students are expected to challenge, they're not expected to copy down what they are told. If they can get up in class and say, "I think you're wrong; I've got a better idea," that's good. That's what you're supposed to cultivate.

In fact, that's what a good education in the sciences is—for a pretty good reason. If it wasn't, the sciences would die. They survive on challenge, creativity, and new ideas, which often come from young people. Any faculty members who don't learn from their students, there's something wrong with them. That's what education ought to be across the board.

**Suppose someone's getting out of school and thinking about becoming a professor, and they also want to be relevant and contribute to justice. Is becoming a professor a good route to follow or are the pitfalls so bad that they will be incapable of carrying out their goals?**

First of all, remember that no human being is solely a professional. You're also a human being. So you can be an algebraic apologist and do extremely good socially relevant work. At, say, MIT the faculty peace groups, which were not very radical, were mostly scientists/Nobel laureates.

Being a scientist, carpenter, or whatever you want to be does not exclude being a human being. But suppose you want to go into a profession that has immediate human consequences—economics, sociology, history, and so on. It's not excluded, but it will be hard. These are people who go into those profession and do extremely good work but run into filters and barriers.

**What does a person need to do to protect themselves from the loss of their social goals?**

Be honest and have a thick skin. You have to understand what the reaction's going to be. People don't like to be challenged. The sciences are better about it, and, even in the other fields, being a professor can be a very comfortable job. You can be a professor at some Ivy League university and do nothing except write your thesis with more data, more documents. You don't have to bother thinking or seeing students. They never raise interesting questions and you're well-off—much better paid than you ought to be, including me. It's a nice, comfortable life, and they're not going to like it if they're going to be challenged. Say you're an economist—you have a lot of forces pressing against you. Take, say, Obama. When he picked his economic advisors, who'd he pick? Did he pick Nobel laureates who raised a couple of questions? No, he picked the people who created the crisis because Obama's in the pocket of the financial institutions—the ones who put him into power. It's kind of interesting to see how that worked. You can learn a lot about how the political system works just by paying attention to what's on the front pages. The financial institutions are now pretty much the core of the economy, since big changes took place in the 1970s. They preferred Obama to McCain. They were the core of his funding, they got him in, and he was expected to work for them. So that's what the policies are. You bail out Goldman Sachs, pick up the debts of IG [Group]—the whole story. And it led to a lot of popular anger—a lot of it is seriously misdirected, but the anger's understandable.

Here we are bailing out the ones who created the crisis and they're making more profits than ever, giving out big bonuses after we bailed them out. Not just TARP. Meanwhile, we're suffering. For manufacturing workers it's like the Great Depression. One out of six unemployed. So there's anger. Obama's a politician, so he had to respond it. He changed his rhetoric and started talking about greedy bankers and how they shouldn't have big bonuses.

He was taught a lesson very fast—within days. The bankers and financial institutions, and others, announced very publicly that if he kept talking like that, they were going to destroy him. "We funded you and other Democrats and we're not going to keep doing it." Within days Obama conceded. He gave an interview to the business press in which he said that the bankers are really a fine group, they're "my friends." "I speak for the American people when I say they deserve their bonuses because we believe in the free market."

Is that what the American people are saying? People want to tear him to shreds, but he speaks for the American people because we believe that these are great guys and they deserve their bonuses and everything else because we believe in the free market—which he doesn't believe in for a minute. The succession of events was like a caricature of the harshest critique of the political system.

## Economics

**This leads into the next area I want to talk about, which is economics. In your view, what's wrong with the private ownership of the means of production?**

I agree with American working people of the nineteenth century. Wage labor is fundamentally no different from slavery unless it's temporary, which it was for a while in the nineteenth century. We should not have relations of hierarchy, dominance, subordination, centralized control over the means of life. If you have private ownership of the means of production, it means it's not one person; it's an institution, a corporation. Internally it is a totalitarian institution—almost necessarily. There are groups at the top that make the decisions, give orders. People down the hierarchy get the orders and transmit them. At the very bottom you get people who are permitted to rent themselves to survive—that's called a job.

And the outside community is allowed to purchase what's been produced, which is heavily propagandized to make them want to consume it even if they don't want it.

So that's the nature of the system, and that's as close to totalitarianism as you can imagine. It gets even worse because when you get to the corporate system, these are state-created institutions, given great privileges by the state—meaning the public, assuming the system's democratic. Take the very nature of corporations: They're based on what's called "limited liability," meaning if you're a participant in a corporation and the corporation carries out mass murder, the participants aren't guilty of it. So corporate mass slaughter is a huge phenomenon, but it's almost never punished. That's a big gift, and that's just the beginning. After that the state has given massive benefits to corporations. It's now embedded into American law. We saw a very dramatic example in the Supreme Court's decision on *Citizens United v. the Federal Electoral Commission*. The ultra-Right on the court (now called "conservative"), appointed by Bush, managed to railroad through just what they were appointed to oppose, which in effect grants corporations the right to buy elections. They were doing it anyway, but they had to go through all kinds of indirect ways.

Now the court says you can advertise for your candidate right to the end, spending as much money as you want. When it's discussed, it says corporations and unions, but that's a bad joke—it's corporations. And the decision was supported by the ACLU, which presented a brief in favor of it. I kind of understand it in a way. It's based on the idea that goes back a century that corporations are what's called "natural entities."

About a century ago the courts and lawyers shifted to a view of corporations which had been articulated, but was in the background. Though they are state-created legal entities, they are also natural entities—meaning persons. Well, humans of flesh and blood have rights, so corporations do as well. Furthermore, a decision was made, also by the courts, that corporations are identical with managers. So the corporation becomes not workers, not even shareholders; it becomes management which means the management of a corporation is a person with all the rights of persons. In later legislation it becomes much worse. Free-trade agreements (NAFTA, WTO), which don't have much to do with free trade, gave corporations—which means management—rights that go way beyond the rights of persons. So here you have these state-created entities, which get massive public support in all kinds of ways such as research and development, possessing rights way beyond persons. Then came the Supreme Court in 2010 saying that you, the management, can buy elections directly. And the ACLU approved it because that's free speech and, after all, [corporations] are persons. The majority opinion, written by Justice Kennedy, includes the harshest critiques of the media that I have ever seen. It goes far beyond anything I would have written. What Kennedy said is that media corporations like CBS have the right of free speech so why shouldn't General Electric?

That's quite interesting. CBS is given massive gifts from the government—like access to the public airwaves—on the condition that they fulfill the public trust, and that is convey information honestly through opinions and so on. They're often criticized for not meeting the public trust, which they don't. But Kennedy is saying they don't have a public trust because they're like General Electric. Well, General Electric, by law, has a commitment, namely to maximize profit. If an executive of General Electric deviates from that, he or she is actually breaking the law. So what Kennedy is saying is that CBS, the NYT, and so on have no public trust. There not supposed to present news, just make profit. They are parts of what's called a free enterprise system—it's a bad joke.

Getting back to your question: Once you have private ownership of the means of production, then that's the way it's going to go almost automatically in the US. The US has a highly class-conscious business class. If you read the business literature, it's like reading Mao's *Red Book*. The values may be inverted, but the terminology is the same. They're fighting a bitter class war constantly. They never relax for a minute. You can't criticize them for doing it as it's their job and they're legally bound to make a profit for power. These are aspects of private enterprise based on an intolerable principle—hierarchy and domination.

**There was this thing that came along called socialism, which still exists in some places but has disappeared in others. What's happened?**
Depends what you mean. If you mean Leninism, then socialism was just another form of tyranny. Lenin didn't hide it particularly. In fact, in the early twentieth century—years before the revolution—Lenin was harshly criticized within the socialist movement because his doctrine was that there should be a dictatorship of the proletariat, a Marxist notion that to Marx meant something quite different—like producers take over. So Lenin said there should be a dictatorship of the proletariat that should be

run by the party, and the party should be run by the Central Committee, and the Central Committee should be run by Lenin. He didn't put it in those words, but that's essentially what it came down to. And all for the "best of reasons," of course.

If you look at Lenin's writings, he veers away from this in early 1917. So from around April 1917, he became much more libertarian—this was during the popular revolution. If you read his thesis on state and revolution it's essentially an anarchist text. Then he got power and went back to his early doctrine. One of his first acts was to take away the power of the Soviets—the factory councils, any of the popular institutions that developed during the revolutionary period. He dismantled the constituent assembly because they were social revolutionaries representing the peasants and finally turned the place into what was called a labor army, and "We've got to drive them to industrialization." It was all from a particular reading of Marx that the proletariat is the engine of social change to freedom and justice, but that it can't happen unless we have an industrial society. But it was a backward peasant society. Marx himself was very interested in the evolutionary potential of the peasantry. In his last years, he worked a lot on it. But all that was suppressed by the urban socialists.

The picture was that we have to industrialize the country in order to have an urban proletariat. Then the iron law of history will start working and you will get socialism, communism, and all kinds of wonderful things. All very progressive. Tolstoy went along with it, and what they developed was tyranny—for "principled reasons." Stalin turned it into a monstrosity, but I think the basic financial structure was already there.

Okay, that's what was called socialism. Now you have two major propaganda systems in the world. The highest by far is the Western propaganda system. The other, which came after 1917, was the Bolshevik propaganda system. It was nowhere near as powerful as the West, but it had a lot of appeal, especially in the Third World. Intellectuals liked it for all kinds of reasons.

These two systems disagreed on a lot of things, but they agreed on one thing, namely, that this was socialism. The West agreed on it because they wanted to defame socialism as tyranny. The Bolsheviks liked it because they wanted to benefit from the moral appeal of the situation. When the world's two propaganda systems agree on something, it's kind of hard to disentangle yourself from it. So it became really existing socialism and it's probably the worst blow that socialism faced, maybe up to Hitler.

In 1988–89, the Russian system was finally collapsing. I was asked by a leftist journalist, "What does it mean?" I said this is a small victory for socialism and then explained why. They refused to publish it. It finally appeared in an anarchist journal in Montreal. I actually wrote something for a symposium in the *Nation*, but I don't think anyone understood what I was saying—even the people who were strong anti-Stalinists. Well, I think what I wrote was true. You know, out of the Marxist movement came another strain—strict Marxists had another position. They were opposed to Bolshevism. In fact, Lenin had a famous pamphlet about them calling the ultra-Left "an infantile disorder." That strain was left-wing Marxism and was not very far from anarcho-syndicalism.

A lot of these people were in favor of the Spanish Revolution—an anarchist revolution. So there was a strain in Russia that wanted workers control in the factories, elimination of the Party hierarchy; very anti-Leninist. But that disappeared and never even reached the West until the 1950s.

Then there were the left-libertarian movements—anarchists, anarcho-syndicalist, and others. But they didn't become socialism. What socialism became was either Leninism or Social Democracy. German Social Democracy was kind of a reformist, parliamentary social democracy, which did things for workers' rights and women's rights, but within the framework of state capitalist democracy.

**What does the word "class" mean to you?**
It has a history, but if you take a look at society, there are different roles people play. There are people who give orders and people who take orders, and it gets institutionalized. So, for example, take the corporate system again. There are directors and the banks that own them and basically set the framework. There are managers who work out how to apply things and give orders, and then you go down the line. They're not totally passive, they can strike, but the array of decision-making control is fairly sharp. Those are classes.

**By virtue of the role they play in the economy.**
You use different terms for other kinds of hierarchy and domination like the patriarchal family. Maybe the father gives the orders, the mother carries out the orders, and the kids do what they're told. We don't call that class, but it's an illustration of the same kind of structural relations.

**Is classlessness possible in an economy?**
That's kind of like asking if slavery is necessary. You go back to the eighteenth century and you ask people how you can have society without slavery. You look around and there are slaves everywhere. Further, it appears to be benevolent. In fact, slave-owners argued that they were more benevolent than Northern manufacturers. "When you own a slave," they said, "you have capital and you want to take care of your capital. Northern manufacturers just rent people, they have no responsibility toward them and can throw them out if they want and get others."

In fact, that's revealed itself dramatically in American history in a period that's kind of suppressed, although we have the information. You're taught in school that slavery ended after the Civil War, and it did, for about ten years. By 1877, there was a compact made by North and South that the South could do what it felt like, so they reinstituted slavery, but they reinstated it in a much more brutal form.

What they did was criminalize black life. If a black man was standing on a street corner, he could be arrested for vagrancy. If he looks at a white woman, he could be arrested for attempted rape. And it didn't matter if you were in jail for a ten-dollar fine, you couldn't get out because you couldn't pay the corrupt judge or lawyer. It was essentially permanent servitude. The criminalized blacks were then handed over to industry, and that's a large part of American industrial development. There was big southern industrialization based on mines, steel, and agriculture, so blacks went back to the cotton fields. This was a large part of our economic history, and it was worse than slavery for exactly the reasons that the slave owners had always argued. So you had a period that was worse than slavery that continued right up to World War II.

During World War II, they needed what was called "free labor" for wartime industry. Blacks got out of criminalized slavery, and then there was the postwar boom, which took place in the 1950s and 1960s, and there were decent jobs for black men in the auto factories.

By the 1970s, that was over. There were social and economic decisions made to deindustrialize the country and turn it into a financial center. If you go back to 1970, the role of financial institutions in the GDP was roughly 3 percent. Now it's a third, and that changes all sorts of things, including sending industry out of the country.

Two years ago the head of IBM testified before Congress. He said that in the early years what was good for American corporations was good for the country. Now what's good for corporations is bad for the country. IBM is a perfect example. They have something like 70 percent of their employees in India and elsewhere. This is striking because IBM exists because of huge public subsidies. That's how computers were developed. The result is that for poor working people, which means heavily black and later Latino, there are no jobs. So what do you do? Throw them in jail just like after Reconstruction. That's the reason the level of incarceration in the US has shot out of sight—mostly on drug charges—and they become slave labor again.

Getting back to your original question, can we get rid of slavery . . . ?

**That wasn't the original question; it was can we have classlessness?**
Well, was it possible to get rid of slavery? It was possible. There were a lot of pressures that prevented it. But, technically, we didn't have slavery after 1870.

**Do you want to communicate that while it's maybe possible to get rid of classlessness, it's pretty much hopeless?**
Getting rid of slavery was progress, but the kind of improvements you make come up against the people who run and manage society, so we have to keep struggling and we can eliminate class in other ways—worker-owned factories etc. It's a big issue right now along with an economic and environmental crisis. It's agreed across the board that one way the US has to try to deal with this is to overcome our hopelessly backward infrastructure (as compared with Europe and Japan). We have a terrible transportation system that's a wasteful use of fossil fuels. That can't go on. We have to at least catch up to the rest of the industrial world. So we need high-speed rail, for one thing. How do you get high-speed rail? Well, Obama sent his transportation secretary to Spain so he could use US federal taxpayer stimulus to make contracts with Spain to provide the US with high-speed rail. At the very same time, Obama's continuing the deindustrialization project from the 1970s. Close down manufacturing plants and you could imagine massive criticism of the socioeconomic system. Destroying a factory doesn't just mean destroying a factory. It means destroying a workforce and an entire community.

Well, the people who work in those factories could take over the plants and run them and convert them to high-speed rail production. It's a task, but not an unsolvable one. Converting wartime production in the

1940s was a far larger task and it was done successfully. It has to at least be in people's consciousness to be able to think about it and then do it. There are examples of it that came pretty close to working. The most important one was in Youngstown, Ohio, about thirty years ago. The town was based around Youngstown Sheet and Tube. U.S. Steel decided to move somewhere else, closing most steel manufacturing in Youngstown in 1977–1980. There were a lot of protests, strikes, sit downs, community protests. Finally there was an effort to take it to the courts to get them to agree that the community and the workforce could take over a corporate institution that was being dismantled. They lost in the court because they didn't have enough public support. But those kinds of things should be at everyone's fingertips.

If you want high-speed rail, you don't have to go to Spain to buy it with taxpayer money. American workers have the skills, the ability, and the capacity to do it themselves. From some point of view, that's a reformist measure. From another point of view, it's a very radical measure. It's a move toward eliminating a class society.

Sure, they'll fight, but that's true of everything. That's why the business class has been fighting like mad to get rid of things like Social Security.

**Were any serious mistakes made in activists' approaches to the economy?**
The biggest mistake was nonexistence. It's very hard to find left approaches to the economy, except in small groups. Popular forces have to be created. There are examples, after all, even in US history. Take the 1920s, when the labor movement was basically destroyed. Woodrow Wilson, the "great idealist," played a part in destroying the unions, which he hated. There's a famous book of labor history, *The Fall of the House of Labor* by David Montgomery, one of the great labor historians. By the "fall" he meant the 1920s. It was so much gone that right-wing articles in British newspapers couldn't believe how oppressed workers were in the US.

It changed in the 1930s when there was a slow revitalization led by the radicalized AFL and CIO, due to the depression. It took five or six years until there was substantial labor organizing and you had sit-down strikes, which are one step before taking over the factory. As soon as that started up, business got nervous as New Deal legislation got passed, some of which was valuable, some of which was to tamp down what was going on.

We're five or so years into the current recession, and it could happen again. Of course, there are things that existed then that don't exist now.

One of them that we're not supposed to talk about is that there was a Communist Party (CP). It was all tied up with Stalin worship, but for most people in the party that didn't mean that much.

My aunts and uncles were unemployed workers. They were in the CP and didn't give a damn about Russia, they were interested in workers' rights, civil rights, rights for blacks, getting a vacation in the union. The CP was in the forefront of almost anything that was happening, whether it was civil rights, worker organizing, and so on. That was smashed. We call it McCarthyism, but it started before that because the idea that you could have a militant, radical, worker-based force was intolerable to American power. That doesn't exist now, but it can be reconstructed on other terms without worshipping some foreign power.

## SESSION FOUR

# The Political System

**ALBERT:** I have a few questions about the political system. In elections, you sometimes suggest voting for people you are simultaneously critical of, as a lesser evil, as the best one can do in the short term. Then there's also the problem of trying to build long-term institutional resistance, including within the electoral arena, for instance a third party. So how do you weigh the benefits of supporting a liberal corporate candidate who isn't that much better than the other, against supporting a third-party candidate in order to make your choices known?

**CHOMSKY:** I don't think there's a formula. It depends on the particular circumstances. Take, say, 2008. I live in Massachusetts, a safe state in that you know how it's going to turn out in the presidential arena. I felt free to vote for the Green Party, which at least was making some kind of effort to develop a lasting alternative. If I had been in a controversial state, say Pennsylvania, I probably would have voted for Obama because I thought it would be pretty dangerous in the short term to have McCain and Palin in there—not that I liked Obama. Other times I didn't see any point in voting at all. Sometimes there's a point, sometimes there isn't. Depends on the options, the alternatives. For example, if Gore had been elected in 2000, it's not obvious that he would have gone to war in Afghanistan and Iraq. If McCain had been elected in 2008, we wouldn't just have an ultra-Right majority in the Court; we'd have an unbreakable majority. There are a lot of choices like that, but it's not a high-level decision. In the US there's not supposed to be any participation. You push a lever and you go home. That's a serious failure of democracy.

It's striking how it's been achieved to the extent that democracy is almost nonexistent. Take, say, primaries. In a democratic society what would happen is the people in a town would get together in their own organizations and assemblies, take a little time, and work out what they would like to see in the next election, and they'd come up with some sort of program. Then, if a candidate comes to town and wants to talk to them, they would say, "You can come to town and listen to us." The candidate would come and explain what they wanted, and if the candidate gave a convincing reason for supporting these things, the townspeople would consider voting for him or her, or maybe they'd have their own representative. That would be a form of democracy.

What happens is totally different. Nobody meets the candidate in town. The candidate, or the public relations representatives, announce they are coming to town, and they gather people together who sit and listen to how wonderful the candidate is and how they are going to do all kinds of wonderful things—and then go home. That's the opposite of democracy.

Take April 15. In a functioning democracy, that would be a day of celebration, a day you hand in your taxes. You would be saying, okay, we got together, we worked out some plans and programs that we think should be implemented and now we're participating by providing the funding to get these things done. That's a democracy. In the US, April 15 is a day of mourning. It's a day when this alien force—the government—is arriving to steal our hard-earned money and use it for their own purposes. That's a reflection of the fact that the concept of democracy is not even in people's minds. Of course, I'm exaggerating a bit about aliens, but it's pretty close.

**What about voter turnout and why people decide to vote for who they vote for?**
There's a lot of effort to get voter turnout. People vote for all kinds of reasons—some of them quite interesting. There was an election in Massachusetts that people thought had a startling result. It was an election for the US Senate that resulted in giving the Republicans what's called the forty-first seat. That concept alone is interesting. There's two formal political parties—Democrat and Republican. The Republicans have lost almost all pretense of being a traditional political party. They have only one policy: "No." They're like the old Communist Party in that discipline is

almost unanimous no matter what the issue is. As for the Democrats, there are groups called moderate Democrats who are pretty much the ones who used to be called liberal Republicans.

The party alignments have shifted so liberal Republicans have been essentially expelled from the Party and they've switched over to become liberal Democrats, meaning moderate, old-fashioned Republicans. So moderate Democrats go along with the Republicans on all sorts of things. Then there are Democrats that are called Left, who are almost entirely centrist, probusiness. They've agreed to acquire a supermajority on everything. That means that a majority rule can't be clocked unless you have a supermajority and the technique to use is to filibuster, which has been around for a long time and was occasionally used. It's now become like the signing statements. The signing statements are when a president says, "Okay, I'll sign this legislation, but I'm not going to follow it." With Bush it became routine, and Obama has picked it up. The filibusters have become the same. They're just a way for the Party of No to insist on a supermajority. It's got to the point that one Republican, Senator Shelby, announced that he was going to hold up every presidential nomination—and there were around seventy routine nominations for staff, etc.

Scott Brown, the guy elected in Massachusetts, was the forty-first vote so even a supermajority wouldn't work. Now the vote has been described as being a kind of popular rebellion against the "leftist" government "taking over." Of course, that's not what happened.

If you look at the voting, Brown won for two reasons. The affluent suburbs were very much engaged and supportive of Brown. So they were condemning Obama. Even though he was giving them a lot, he was not giving them enough and they wanted more. That's the affluent suburbs. In the urban areas—which are mostly Democratic, working-class, and poor—voter turnout was very low. They were essentially telling Obama, "You're giving everything away. We're not even getting to take part."

Particularly interesting was the union vote. It was lower than usual, but the majority of the union vote went to Brown. It's been discussed in the labor press, like *Labor Notes*, where they interviewed people. Working people were furious about the health care program. And the vote was portrayed as a critique of the health care system when, in fact, people don't like the health care program because it doesn't go far enough. A considerable majority of the population preferred the public option, Medicare, and other things Obama eventually canned. In the case of the union leaders, activists, and working people, they were furious because Obama had agreed to everything except an excise tax on Cadillac plants. These are what working people have succeeded in eking out of their employers through the unions in a trade-off in the class war. This was a bad error of the unions from way back—to give up almost everything, but at least get some benefit for their people, not for others, just for their own. It's one of the reasons we don't have a national health care program. It's because of the focus of the union on themselves, unlike Canada which insisted on health care for everybody. In the US, they bought into the corporate system and got health care for their union members only.

The result is that unionized workers get pretty decent—by US standards—health care plans, and Obama insists on taxing them heavily. So they were furious and voted for Brown. They were, of course, shooting themselves in the foot, but the voting is understandable.

**The anger is justified. The willingness to rebel is justified, it's just that there's no avenue to do anything except make it worse.**
And that generalizes over the country. I've been saying for some time—and other people have too—that it's a serious mistake for the Left to make fun of the Tea Party movement—Sarah Palin and the rest of them. Sure, it's easy to make fun of them because it is kind of comical, but that's not the point. What we should be doing is ridiculing ourselves. These are people who ought to be organized by the Left. There are all kinds of groups—some very far to the right—but I think at the core of it, there are legitimate grievances. These are people who've worked hard all their lives, they've done everything they're supposed to do, and they're being shafted and have been for thirty years or more. Wages have stagnated or declined, benefit services have collapsed. They were never very good. Schools are lousy, so what's happening to us and why is it happening? Well, they get an answer from, say, Glenn Beck, that the rich liberals are taking everything, they don't care about working people, and they give it away to illegal immigrants. So this is a coherent answer, and they accept it. Liberal Democrats aren't going to give them an answer. They're not going to say that this is happening to you because for the last thirty years we've been working with the corporate system to deindustrialize society and enrich banks. They're not going to hear that, and the Left is not telling them anything. It's trying to, but it's just not reaching them.

That's extremely dangerous. It has the whiff of the Weimar Republic to it. So it's like the unions in Massachusetts shooting themselves in the foot has become clear right away. As soon as Brown was elected, he managed—with help from so-called moderate Democrats—to be in time to help block an appointment to the National Labor Relations Board (NLRB), the only prounion appointment to likely get into the NLRB.

**If you go back to the late 1960s and you come all the way forward, in those fifty years, there's been people critical of all these things you're talking about. If we are honest about it, we haven't produced an awareness or a mechanism that speaks to the broad population, even at a time when the population is furious at the government, at employers, at Wall Street, and so on. Either we've been doing something wrong or it's hopeless. It would be much better if we had just made mistakes. In trying to improve the political system and raise political consciousness for activism in the broad population, what should have or shouldn't have been done?**
Right now the Left is just a conglomeration of a lot of people who are very scattered and issue-oriented. Part of the Left is dedicated to gay rights, another part is dedicated to environmental issues, another is concerned with nuclear weapons. There are a whole lot of issues that tend to be separated. You can't really identify an organized Left that's addressing the kinds of concerns that the general population very rightly has. What part of the Left has been talking constantly, clearly to the right people about the fact that financialization of the economy from the 1970s has led to stagnation, basically, of real wages along with the deterioration of limited benefits.

In fact, a large part of the issue-oriented Left, unfortunately, has alienated the population. We may not like it, but the fact is that a large part of the population is racist, sexist, and opposed to gay rights. While working on those issues is correct, it's got to be done in a way that recognizes the reality of the audience that's out there.

**Moving to one of those issues, what is race?**
First of all, here the postmodernists are right: It's a social construction. We decide there are different races. There are a lot of ways to categorize people. We do it by "color" or hairstyle or whatever it is. It's a deep stain in American history. It goes right back to slavery, which I've already talked

about. It sets up very strikingly in people's attitudes which are quite different from what is usually claimed.

One of the things that political scientists do pretty well is study popular attitudes by extensive polling. They publish interesting results. The current issue of their *Political Science Quarterly* has an article reviewing a lot of poll studies on attitudes to social justice. The results are interesting. It turns out that, contrary to what is commonly claimed, the population is basically socially democratic in their attitudes. Interestingly, the author identifies those who call themselves antigovernment. Just looking at their attitudes, they tend to be in favor of more federal spending for education and social security. But there are two exceptions: They think we're giving too much to blacks and too much to people on welfare. It has no relation to reality, but we can see where it comes from—unremitting propaganda that's based on traditional racism and on the Reaganite type of extremist propaganda about "welfare mothers in their black Cadillacs coming to steal your money." You have enough propaganda like that and you get this split in attitudes. Remember, we're talking about people who regard themselves as antigovernment, i.e. right-wing.

In the general population, it's similar, but less striking in a way. Actually when you ask people (they didn't happen to in these polls), "What do you think we ought to give poor mothers with dependent children?" Their answers are to give way more than we actually do, and the same with foreign policy aid too.

When you ask them what they think about foreign aid, they say we're giving it all away to those undeserving people. When you ask what they think we ought to give them, it's ten times more than we actually do. What I think it means is that the audience is there because people's attitudes are more or less social democratic.

**Do you believe global warming is largely human-made? I ask the question because there are a number of people who would say no.**
I don't have any particular technical expertise, but I don't see the slightest reason to doubt the evidence that's been presented or to question the overwhelming concerns of scientists. So, yes, I take it for granted that it's anthropogenic.

**How do you understand the seeming unwillingness of governments and of those people who are in a position to prevent the likely calamity?**

My feeling is that CEOs of most corporations, like ExxonMobil or General Electric, have about the same beliefs as college professors on most things, so they know it's happening.

Their standard answer is that they're concentrating on short-term problems and they have to make sure the bottom line is good enough or else they lose their salaries—that sort of thing. That part is true, but you go deeper and it gets back to what we were talking about before. This is part of a market economy. By the way, we don't really have a market economy, it's kind of a quasi-market economy, but there are market elements in the economy.

Among these market elements is that you simply have to pursue short-term interests or else you're out. Suppose there are three car companies—Ford, GM, and Chrysler. Imagine they're comparable, and suppose one of them says, "We're going to devote resources to making better cars ten years from now because that's how market systems work." To the extent that there is limited competition, which there is, you're compelled to focus on short-term gains greater than the others or you're out of the game.

Take, say, the financial crisis. The economists talk about how they didn't pay enough attention to systemic risk. Of course, this was pointed out ten years ago.

Two pretty well-known economists—John Eatwell and Lance Taylor—wrote a book *Global Finance at Risk* where they pointed out that because systemic risk isn't considered—it's an externality—there's going to be a catastrophe. You're underpricing risk, so of course it will crash. It's built into the system.

If, say, you and I make a good deal for ourselves, but we're not paying attention to the effect on somebody else—like congestion, pollution, and gas prices—then this is one of the inefficiencies of markets.

**This explains why the powerful people in the economy, regardless of their desires, can't do anything to deal with global warming.**
What they do is interesting. Take BP: They're trying to buy into the alternative technology market, figuring that's going to be a profitable market. Tom Ferguson did a lot of studies on the New Deal. What he found is that during the New Deal, Roosevelt was getting support from a particular section of industry—high-tech, internally oriented industry. Gerard Swope, head of GE, was quite strongly in favor of the New Deal. On the other hand, they were passionately opposed to low-tech, labor intensive,

domestic-oriented industry. For just that reason, capital intensive GE, wanted a disciplined workforce.

**I could imagine a president marshalling the bully pulpit to educate people on the crisis of global warming. You could imagine, as a result, a powerful upsurge which would create a context in which the market dynamic is overwhelmed and you get some results.**
It happened. Al Gore tried and he was smashed. He was denounced as a liberal elitist, out of touch; he takes jet planes, after all. There are always strong counterforces, and defamation is one of the easiest things to do. You can make up lies as much as you want. You can make people look ridiculous. It could have worked, but it would require a lot of popular organization.

Actually, Roosevelt did it to a limited extent. But he had a mass popular movement behind him. The labor movement really did organize, and there were plenty of other movements. The country became pretty radical. So you had a basis to go after the bankers and institute some reasonable legislation—Glass-Steagall, Social Security, the Wagner Act, and others.

**Another issue of concern over the years that has caused some friction among activists is vegetarianism. Do you think there's a moral case for it?**
Yes, I think there is a moral case for it. I get a ton of letters on the issue. But there's a moral case for a lot of things. For instance, if you look at human deaths from starvation and death among young children, there are about twice as many in the US as in Rwanda. You can decide to deal with them both—vegetarianism and starvation—and many of the other problems, but time is limited, which means you have to pick and choose because you can't do all of them. You have to set priorities. In this case, if I have a choice between devoting my time trying to save the children or trying to stop the mass genocide of domestic animals, I'll save the children.

While vegetarianism is an effort to reduce animal suffering, suppose we all became vegetarians. The first thing you'd have to do is eliminate almost all domesticated animals because they are raised to eat. They'll starve to death if you don't feed them. Do you get rid of them, let them proliferate? These are consequences of vegetarianism.

**Do you think that many people putting lots of time into their concern for animals, not humans, indicates that they feel they can succeed on this front?**

They can't succeed on vegetarianism. Look, I don't want to criticize particular groups of people. They make their choices. Maybe it's a sensible choice in their lives.

**Another thing you encounter as an organizer is the person who feels the deck is stacked, that what you do has no efficacy, no possibility of succeeding, so why bother.**
History doesn't tell you that. What history tells you is that a lot of things have been overcome. State repression exists, but it is nothing like it's been in the past. It's extremely unlikely that the government can carry out anything like President Wilson's Red Scare or even COINTELPRO. They can do things, but they've lost the ability to use force, and we know it and they know it. That's one of the reasons for the development of public relations and the modern propaganda system. Systems of power knew, in fact said, that they had lost the ability to control people in the US by violence. So they'll control us in other ways by controlling opinion and attitude. It even shows up in financial institutions as it becomes harder to impose on the population the costs of the market system.

So after World War II, when the Bretton Woods system was set up, they instituted control over capital movement and speculation as a way of compensating for the inability to distribute the cost of market systems to the public. That's why we had a few decades of growth. With the breakdown in the 1970s, you get the costs.

# SESSION FIVE

# International Relations

**ALBERT:** What does colonialism mean?

**CHOMSKY:** Like any term about human affairs, it covers a vast range. There are all kinds of colonialism. The worst kind is what's called "settler colonialism," like the US, Australia, and Israel. Settler colonialism means you exterminate the indigenous population, maybe not 100 percent, but pretty close. So that's the absolute worst colonialism—and that's the US There are other kinds of colonialism that are less extreme. Take the case of Haiti: You take over a country for your own benefit, get as much as you can out of it, destroy the agricultural system, and starve the population into the cities—all, of course, claimed to be done for the most "beneficial" reasons.

There are other kinds. Take the US and the Philippines, which happened to be an innovation in imperial history. The US invaded the Philippines about a century ago. It killed a couple of hundred thousand people. It was vicious racism. People in the US weren't even sure Filipinos were humans. They were considered apes and were exhibited at international fairs. It was horrendous when you look back at it. Of course, it was all done for the most "noble" reasons as we were uplifting and Christianizing them, giving them civilization—the usual. There were scattered opponents to what the US was doing in the Philippines. Mark Twain wrote very sardonic and cutting anti-imperialist essays. He wasn't hanged, but the essays were repressed. I think they finally came out around twenty years ago in some scholarly edition that nobody ever read. But he wrote them, and there was an anti-imperialist league at the time as well.

So what happened after the US conquered the Philippines? It was recently studied in a book by Alfred McCoy, a historian of the Philippines, among other achievements. Turns out there was a major innovation which had a lot of consequences right up to today. What was instituted was a very sophisticated, high-tech control and surveillance system. Of course, the technology was not the technology of today, but there was telegraph, radio, etc. Every available technique was used—co-optation of elites, spreading rumors, using every device to undermine the nationalists. It was done very well, and, of course, there's a fist in the background—the Philippine Constabulary. That's what happens in every colonial imperial system. You have a paramilitary force of collaborators who do what you tell them. They're usually trained killers. You can set it up so you recruit people of one tribe to kill another tribe or use the rural population to smash the urban population. It's done in various ways. In fact, that's the way the US is hoping to run the occupied Palestinian territories. There's a US-run army that's supposed to subdue them. It's praised by Obama, Kerry, and the liberals.

Anyway, this array of techniques was worked out in quite impressive detail and applied in a sophisticated fashion. It still applies. The Philippines, which remains a kind of quasi-colony, is the only part of Southeast Asia that has not been part of the so-called economic miracle— Taiwan, South Korea, Indonesia—there's been a lot of economic development. Not in the Philippines. It's the one part of the region that the US still runs. Many of the techniques used in the Philippines were later applied domestically by President Wilson, as well as the British during World War I. They were used consciously. Now it's extreme. You go to Britain and it's a surveillance society with cameras on every street corner. In the US we have the PATRIOT Act. We also applied them in other countries right away—Haiti, the Dominican Republic, Nicaragua. That's another kind of colonialism. It makes a lot more sense than occupying the country. It's cheaper. It can work effectively. In the Philippines it's worked for one hundred years and has provided techniques to use back home in the US for controlling and subduing the population.

To get back to your question, colonialism is one form with which powerful systems subdue others and their own populations. There's nothing new about it. Adam Smith pointed out that if you want to know how a country works, you cannot ignore the domestic distribution of power. He pointed out in *The Wealth of Nations* that you have to recognize that the architects of policy are merchants and manufacturers, and they set policies in which their interests are well dealt with, even though (in Smith's case) the people of England may be grievous. Of course, elsewhere it's even worse. For instance, the British Empire affected not only the population of India, but the population of England, which was also kind of colonized. So it's class war.

**At the other end of the spectrum, what do you think internationalism means or implies?**
Internationalism should be what it has always been, at least in the terminology of the Left. Unions were called internationals, not because they are international, but because they ought to be. Their initial creation was motivated, in part, by the idea that we ought to be concerned with working people, peasants, and other oppressed people around the world. International solidarity is the ideology of unions. The World Social Forum (WSF) today is about as close as there is to the internationals. If it weren't so caught up in crazy ideology, we'd call the WSF the one proglobalization group in the world. It's not Davos, where you get a lot of rich people talking about how to enrich themselves; that is called globalization. The World Social Forum brings together people from all over the world, all walks of life, and mutually interacting and sharing supportive ideas about how to improve the world for the vast majority. That's internationalism. We should be doing it. And anti-imperialism is a form of internationalism.

**When do you think it's right for an individual in the US to denounce human rights in another country and when do you think it's hypocrisy or interference?**
Again, it's a question of priorities. If there are human rights violations somewhere, it makes sense to criticize them if you can do something about them. If you can't do anything about them, it's just posturing. But if you can help human rights activists or oppressed people somewhere else, you should do it. The question is always priorities. Time and energy are finite, and the question is how we decide to distribute our energies when there are human rights violations.

What you prioritize is what any moral human being does: the predictable consequence of your own actions. That's what should be prioritized. The one thing you can't improve is what you are doing. So, overwhelmingly, our priorities ought to be our engagement in human rights violations, which we can change. Incidentally, that's independent of scale. Even if the ones the US is carrying out are not so terrible and the ones someone else is carrying out are awful, but we can't do anything about it. Elementary morality says let's focus on ourselves. The practice is almost 100 percent the reverse.

Furthermore, it's kind of irreversible. Great pleasure is taken in the crimes of others, especially if we can't do anything about them. If some enemy commits horrible crimes and we can't do anything about it, it's irresistible to posture heroically about their crimes. For one thing it's costless because you can't do anything about it; for another thing it shows how noble you are. Another thing is you can lie like a trooper. You can say anything you want.

## Self-Determination

If anybody says that's not quite accurate, you can come back and say, oh, you're a genocide supporter or you're in favor of Holocausts. There's a whole stream of techniques available. Intellectuals just love it. Castigating ourselves for not criticizing strongly enough the crimes of others. That's just marvelous. For one thing, you're criticizing yourself, so look how moral you are. And you're criticizing us for not doing enough about the crimes of enemies, which we can't do much about.

If you look at the literature on this, it's astonishing. It's carried out almost to a T. It's like a caricature of itself. The people are nice people, but they think that we ought to castigate ourselves for not doing enough about, say, Pol Pot's genocide, even though there was no suggestion about what to do about it. Meanwhile, we totally ignore what the US is doing.

### What sort of a right is self-determination?

I don't think you can give a blanket answer. It depends on circumstances. From one point of view, everyone has the right of self-determination. You have a right to control your own life. On the other hand, self-determination is not done in isolation. It has consequences for others, so you have to take that into account. You have to start balancing things.

Take secession in the South in the US. Should Southerners have the right of self-determination? Well, who is asking for self-determination? White Southerners, not black slaves. So it was asking for self-determination for a large part of the Southern population. I do not see how there can be formulas about this because, while it is a value, it is only one of many values. As in all human affairs, generally, values often conflict.

**Do you have views about new international structures that might better protect the weak and the poor?**
I'm pretty much in the mainstream of American public opinion on this and totally different from elite opinion. I've written about it and reviewed the polls. A considerable majority of the public thinks that the UN, not the US, ought to take the lead on international crises. A majority of the population thinks the US out to give up the veto on the Security Council and follow the will of the majority.

A few years ago, a considerable majority agreed with almost the entire world that Iran had the right to enriched uranium. This was before a huge propaganda campaign. What we read in the US was that Iran was defying the world by some interesting definition of "the world," which means the US government and whoever happens to agree with us. It excludes the majority of the population of the US. It includes the nonaligned countries, which is most of the world. A large majority opposed threats of force against Iran. That is, they opposed the US being a rogue, outlaw state, which violates the UN Charter. The UN Charter, although nobody will mention it, bars the threat of force in international affairs, meaning everybody in the American political system is a criminal because, across the board, all options have to be open. About 80 percent of the population thought the US should live up to its legal obligation—legally determined by the World Court—and observe the nonproliferation treaty, meaning making good faith efforts to eliminate nuclear weapons.

The most interesting vote in this connection is that a huge percentage thought we should establish a nuclear-weapons-free zone in the Middle East. That's the right answer to the problems, such as they are. Technically, the US says yes, but there's nothing being done about it.

If you're really interested in nonproliferation, like Obama claims he is, you'd support nuclear-weapons-free zones. They're steps toward decreasing the threat of nuclear proliferation. The facts are extremely revealing. With regard to the Middle East, there's popular support around the world. What that would mean is no nuclear weapons in Iran, Israel, or US forces deployed there. That would be a nuclear-weapons-free zone. That's why it's not on the agenda, except for the population. It would be an important step. It's technically feasible and it would eliminate some of the danger, but it's not on the agenda. Also not mentionable is that the US and Britain happen to have a very strong commitment to this.

The reason is because of something unutterable. When the US and Britain went to war with Iraq, they tried to provide a thin legal cover for it. What they appealed to was Security Council Resolution 687 from 1991, which called on Iraq to eliminate its weapons of mass destruction. And the story was they had none, so we had no right to invade. If you read the resolution, it calls for a nuclear free zone in the Middle East. Therefore, the US and Britain, way more than any other country, are committed to this. It gets more interesting. There are nuclear-weapons-free zones in the world. One was finally achieved in Africa after a lot of negotiations. It's being blocked by the US. The reason is that the African Union regards the island of Diego Garcia in the Indian Ocean as part of Africa because it's part of Mauritius, which is part of the African Union. Britain, under US orders, kicked out the whole population, illegally, some years ago in order to build a big US military base. So Britain didn't accept the African Union agreement. The US refused to accept it, so the US is blocking the African Union nuclear-free zone because we insist on keeping a military base after kicking out the population to store nuclear weapons and, critically, for bombing. It's one of the main bases for carrying out aggression in Central Asia and the Middle East. They bombed Iraq from there. Just a couple of weeks ago, the Navy announced they're sending a submarine tender to Diego Garcia to service nuclear submarines.

So the US blocked a nuclear free zone and refused to even talk about a Middle East zone. And there's more. There's a South Pacific nuclear-weapons-free zone. It was held up for a long time by the French because they wanted to use the French Islands for nuclear weapons testing. They finally did their testing, and now it's being held up by the US because the Pacific Islands are used for nuclear weapons storage and nuclear submarines. Meanwhile, Obama is giving highly praised speeches about how awful nuclear weapons are, while there's massive pretend concern about Iran's developing nuclear weapons.

If anyone from Mars was watching this, they'd be amazed that the species can even go on. How can you do all this without collapsing with ridicule about ourselves? Well, it's easy in a well-disciplined society. The interesting thing is that there are novelists who try to describe it—Joseph Heller, Kurt Vonnegut—and they're read and people laugh, but they don't realize their reality.

**What mistakes to you think the antiwar movement has made? What should we have done differently?**
There are a lot of things that could have been done a lot better. For one thing, sectors of the antiwar movement undertook questionable tactics. If you're any kind of an activist, you have to make a distinction between two kinds of tactics—you could call them feel-good tactics; tactics that make you feel good about yourself or when you do something for somebody else. The antiwar movement dissolved to a large extent into feel-good tactics, which were harmful. In fact, the Vietnamese were aware of it. I talked with them. What they liked was quiet, nonviolent demonstrations. What they didn't like was what the Weathermen were doing. Their tactics were understandable from the point of view of the people involved who were frustrated, bitter, and nothing was working so, "Let's go out and smash windows," or, "Let's go out and have a fight in a Third Avenue bar and show the people we're authentic." These were just gifts to the ultra-hawks. They helped build support for the war and it was obvious they were going to have that effect. As the movement dissolved into sectarianism, after 1968, a lot of it was self-destructive.

The other big error was to stop. By 1975, the end of the Vietnam War, about 70 percent of the population had condemned the war as fundamentally wrong and immoral, not a mistake. Those are kind of unbelievable figures because nobody ever said that. Where'd they get it from? What do they even mean? Well it meant there was a huge reservoir of possible support for antiwar activities, but it dissolved, it left. Everybody went away and started condemning the Khmer Rouge for doing some other thing. So then come the Central America massacres, and so it goes on. There are other things. Almost nobody agrees with me. I have friends on the Left, and many of them don't even understand my own view, which goes back to around 1970, that the US won the war. The business world recognized that, but the Left is committed to the doctrine that we won, we stopped the war, or the Vietnamese won, the people united. That's not what happened. We have a rich documentary record that is very instructive. We should think about it and be intellectually honest about it.

The US didn't go to war to conquer Vietnam. In fact, it didn't care if Vietnam dropped off the planet. It went to war for the usual reason—the Mafia principle. It's the dominant principle in world affairs. The Godfather does not accept disobedience. It's dangerous. If one country gets away with disobedience, no matter how tiny it is, somebody else will get the idea and pretty soon the whole system erodes. Vietnam was a case in point. The US was afraid that Vietnam's nationalism would be successful, that you'd have successful economic development. It would, to use Kissinger's terminology, be a virus that would spread contagion to Thailand, Malaysia, and Indonesia. And now you're in trouble, as Indonesia has real resources. Then, pretty soon, maybe ultimately, Japan, which historian John Dower called the "super domino." Japan would accommodate to an independent Asia and Southeast Asia.

It would become its technological and military center which would mean that the US would have lost the Pacific phase of World War II. In 1950, we weren't ready to lose World War II. So you have a "virus" that's spreading contagion. There's a cure: Destroy the virus and inoculate the potential victims. It was done. South Vietnam was pretty much destroyed by 1965, the rest of Indochina not long afterwards. It would never be a model of independent development. The surrounding countries were inoculated by vicious dictatorships. The most important was Indonesia. In 1965, the Suharto coup was met with total euphoria by the US. A million people were killed, the mass popular organizations were destroyed, and the country was opened up to the West. No more accommodation, no more contagion.

McGeorge Bundy—Kennedy's national security advisor—was no fool. In retrospect, he said we should have stopped the war in 1965. He was right. Vietnam was already essentially destroyed. Indonesia, the big prize, was inoculated and they had a vicious military dictatorship—"our kind of guy," as Bill Clinton called him. Japan was on our side, so what was the point. It's a waste of time.

The antiwar movement should understand that, because there's a pattern that is followed over and over. The domino theory is sometimes ridiculed, but everybody believes it because it's true. The world's mostly run like the Mafia. If you don't understand that, you're not going to understand the next thing that happens in the world. That's part of the reason for the incredible antagonism to Iran. Why Iran? It has a terrible government, but there are a lot of terrible governments. Saudi Arabia is a lot worse.

Well, Iran was disobedient. It took hostages. How can we let them get away with that? Cuba is a striking example. For decades, the majority of the US population has been in favor of normalizing relations with Cuba. Disregarding the population is normal, but the business world is in favor of it and has been for a long time. Big sectors like agribusiness, pharmaceuticals—really powerful sectors. But we can't do it. We've got to keep punishing them because they were disobedient.

**When you encounter the extent of horror in the world, how do you get through all that and then go to work?**
Actually, going back to work is one of the cures for it. If there's nothing you can think of doing, you just collapse. You may decide to give up or go into a deep depression. If you can keep working, that's a cure.

**You have an advantage, though. When you write or speak, you must know that it's having an impact. There are many people working for justice who feel they have no impact and they feel crushed.**
Realistically there's very little impact, but I feel I'm doing the right thing, and if it reaches some people, okay. The same is true of any organizer. You organize people in a community to get a traffic light installed where kids cross the street. They achieved something. It empowers people and they go on to the next thing. It's not hopeless.

**Over the years, you've been subject to intense scrutiny. People attack you and attribute views to you that you don't hold or describe them so they are unrecognizable.**
I get that all the time. People lie, slander, and vilify. Sometimes the attacks are of interest. They are correct ones, so I learn something. Those are extremely rare. But you have to ask yourself, "Am I getting assassinated by an elite army battalion trained at Fort Bragg?" That's what happens to activists in US domains. Is it happening to me? No.

**What were your views about Cambodia and why do you think they elicited the attacks?**
First of all, I've been quite interested in this. I didn't write anything myself in those days; I wrote with Edward Herman. There has been a huge literature trying to show something wrong with what we wrote. It's literally the case that nobody found a misplaced comma.

**You mean the stuff you wrote about Cambodia?**
It has to be the best stuff ever written because anything you write has some mistakes. If you read the professional journals, the last paragraph of every review of a scholarly monograph lists the errors. Literally nothing

on the material on Cambodia, and the reason was explained quite early on. What we wrote was carefully checked by some of the leading specialists. They went through it and corrected some things, so it's very unlikely there would be mistakes. Second, we didn't explain anything. We claimed almost nothing. We didn't take any position on it. We just said, "Look, here's the data that's available, here's what comes out of the doctrinal system." Let's compare them because we don't know what happened. In fact, we said maybe the most extreme inventions will turn out to be correct. That's not our question; our question was let's compare what went in to what came out. The only way you can make a mistake on that is a logical error. We didn't make any. There were no factual errors because we took the data that was there and that was noticed right away by one of the leading Cambodia historians, David Chandler, who wrote about our monograph, "Look, this is going to stand no matter what's discovered because your claims are so limited." To the extent we took a position at all, we basically repeated what US intelligence was saying. Everyone agreed that they were the most knowledgeable source.

Remember Ed Herman and I wrote two volumes that South End Press published—*The Political Economy of Human Rights*. These two volumes were concerned entirely with how the data that comes in relates to the data that comes out. Almost the entire two volumes are about US crimes. How is the data that we have about them related to what comes out, which turns out to be apologetics and denial. Nobody has ever mentioned any of that. We had two major examples. There's a chapter devoted to Cambodia, which we went through in detail. There's a chapter devoted to East Timor, which we went through in detail. It's a very good comparison—two major atrocities at the same time and place. One was in the course of an invasion and was much worse—East Timor. But the main difference between them was that in one case it was the US's responsibility and we could have stopped it right away. In the other case, it was somebody else's atrocity, which we could do nothing about.

I don't think there's ever been a word about the chapter on East Timor, the one that's vastly more important. First of all, it's our crime, it's a huge one, and we could have stopped it. Therefore, silence, except for some words of denial. Mostly, it was avoidance.

On Cambodia there's been an intense effort to try to show something wrong with what Ed and I wrote. Well, that tells you something. It illustrates what we talked about before. The actual practice of intellectuals gives you extremely good criteria for what should be done by a person with elementary moral convictions, namely, the opposite of what is always done.

It continues right to the present. In fact, I happened to answer a few questions about it. In answering, I pointed these two things out. I also pointed out that if you say that you're concerned about the Cambodian bombing, okay, it's good that you're concerned about that. How about being concerned about the new revelations about the incredible scale of the US attack on Cambodia which, in fact, created the Khmer Rouge, which you are upset about. Why don't you ask something about that? The response was interesting. Not one word about it, as if I never said it. In *Manufacturing Consent*, ten years later, we reviewed what had happened and what happened since. The effect? Zero. The only thing they noticed about the book is that they think it's about press conspiracy theories.

**You've talked about 9-11 and the Kennedy assassination. You've also been slammed for your views on the Mideast—been called an anti-Semite and a self-hating Jew. What are your views and why do you think they elicited such attacks?**

The attacks are quite interesting. They have a long history. They go back to the Bible. The phrase "self-hating Jew" comes from the book of Kings. The epitome of evil in the Bible was King Ahab, the evil king. At one point he called the prophet Elijah to him and asked Elijah "Why are you a hater of Israel?" What did he mean? He meant that Elijah was condemning the acts of the evil king. And the king, like every totalitarian, identified himself with the culture and society of Israel. So if Elijah was condemning King Ahab's crimes, then he must be a hater of Israel. That's the origin of the phrase "self-hating Jew". It runs through history, and in the modern period it is very explicit. Abba Eban, an Israeli diplomat—highly respected, British accent, a leading liberal humanist. He wrote an article thirty-five years ago in the *American Jewish Congress Weekly* in which he told American Jews that their task was "to show that critics of Zionism" (he meant critics of the state of Israel) fall into two categories: anti-Semitic and neurotic, self-hating Jews. This covers 100 percent of the criticism. If it's from non-Jews, it's anti-Semitism. If it's from Jews, they're self-hating. He mentioned two examples: me and I.F. Stone, who is a dedicated Zionist. Abba Eban picked us because we were criticizing things and he gave the game away just as King Ahab had done and plenty of people in between.

There's a counterpart to that, which nobody seems to notice, and that's the concept of anti-American. We're back to King Ahab. It's a straight totalitarian concept. It's used in totalitarian states like the Soviet Union. Critics were called anti-Soviet. Were they against the Russian people and culture? On the contrary. They were critics of the crimes of a totalitarian state. I know of only one democracy which adopts this totalitarian concept—the United States.

Suppose some people in Italy condemned Berlusconi and were then called anti-Italian. People would collapse in laughter in the streets of Italy. But in a totalitarian culture, like Western intellectual culture, if you attack the holy state, you must be anti-American. What's quite interesting about the US and England and a large part of Europe is that this totalitarian concept is accepted uncritically, with regard to the US. There are even books called anti-American by people who are considered liberal scholars. Who are they? They're people who criticize government policy.

# SECTION II
# Chomsky Raps with Michael Albert

In January 1993 Michael Albert and Noam Chomsky recorded a series of conversations which were later distributed by Z *Magazine*. Here we present a transcription of some material from the 1993 tapes, essentially verbatim. Some of the topical material is now historical, of course, but the rest is as timely as when first discussed.

**ALBERT:** You once wrote an essay called "The Responsibility of Intellectuals." Perhaps we could start by talking a little bit about that. First of all, what makes a person an intellectual in the first place? What is an intellectual?

**CHOMSKY:** It's not a term I take all that seriously. Some of the most intellectual people I've met and known in my life were very remote from the so-called intellectual professions. Plenty of people who are called intellectual workers, who work with their minds, not their, say, hands, are involved in what amounts to clerical work. An awful lot of academic scholarship, for example, is basically a kind of clerical work.

**Suppose we use the word positively.**

With a positive connotation I would want to talk about whoever it is who's thinking about things, trying to understand things, trying to work things out, maybe trying to articulate and express that understanding to others and so on. That's intellectual life.

**So "things" could be society, it could be quarks...**

It could be music.

**It could be sports. So basically, arguably, just about everyone.**
Except that an awful lot of the activity of most of us is routine, not considered, not directed to problems that really do concern us and not based on efforts, maybe even opportunities to gain deeper understanding.

**So intellectuals have a whole lot of time to do this part of life that we all do some of the time.**
There are people who are privileged enough to be able to spend an awful lot of their time and effort on these things if they so choose. They rarely do. They often do turn to routine kind of hack work, which is the easy way.

**So supposing a society like ours does give some people the opportunity to spend more time doing intellectual work, then I guess that's the context in which we raise the question, What's the responsibility of a person like that, a person who is free to have that time?**
We can distinguish what we you might call their "task" from their moral responsibility. Their task, that is, the reason why social institutions provide them with this time and effort, their task is, say, so that they can support power, authority, they can carry out doctrinal management. They can try to ensure that others perceive the world in a way which is supportive of existing authority and privilege. That's their task. If they stop performing their task, they're likely to be deprived of the opportunities to dedicate themselves to intellectual work. On the other hand, their moral responsibility is quite different—in fact, almost the opposite. Their moral responsibility is to try to understand the truth, to try to work with others to come to an understanding of what the world is like, to try to convey that to other people, help them understand, and lay the basis for constructive action. That's their responsibility.

But of course there is a conflict. If you pursue the responsibility, you're likely to be denied the privileges of exercising the intellectual effort. It's pretty evident, not hard to understand. If you're a young person, say, in college or in journalism, or for that matter a fourth grader, and you have too much of an independent mind, meaning you're beginning to fulfill your responsibility, there is a whole variety of devices that will try to deflect you from that error and, if you can't be controlled, to marginalize and eliminate you some way. In fourth grade you may be a behavior problem. In college you may be irresponsible and erratic and not the right kind of student. If you make it to the faculty you'll fail in what's sometimes called "collegiality": getting along with your colleagues. If you're a young journalist and you're pursuing stories that the managerial level above you understands, either intuitively or explicitly, are not to be pursued, you can be sent off to the police desk and advised that you are not thinking through properly and how you don't have proper standards of objectivity and so on. There's a range of devices. We live in a free society, so you're not sent to the gas chambers. They don't send the death squads after you, as is commonly done in many countries. You don't have to go very far away to see that, say, in Mexico. But there nevertheless are quite successful devices to ensure that doctrinal correctness is not seriously infringed upon.

**But certainly intellectuals aren't only journalists, economists, political scientists, and the like. That's one set in the social sciences. But then there's also hard scientists. There's biologists and physicists and the like. There it would seem that there's less of a social control problem, and so maybe you get a different kind of behavior. Are the intellectuals in the linguistics department comparable to the intellectuals in the economics department?**
First of all, there is a social control problem. It's just that we've transcended it. Galileo faced it, for example. You go back a couple of centuries in the West and the social control problem was very severe. Descartes is alleged to have destroyed the final volume of his treatise on the world, the one that was supposed to deal with the human mind, because he learned of the fate of Galileo. That's something like the death squads. The Inquisition was doing precisely that. Okay, that's past, in the West, at least. Not everywhere.

**Why is it past? In other words, what is it about a society in the West that enables at least that kind of pursuit of knowledge to be free to go wherever it goes, but not in, say, Muslim society?**
There are a number of reasons. One of them is just increase in freedom and enlightenment. We've become a much freer society than we were in absolutist times. Popular struggles over centuries have enlarged the domain of freedom. Intellectuals have often played a role in this, during the Enlightenment for example, in breaking barriers and creating a space for greater freedom of thought. That often took a lot of courage and quite a struggle. And it goes on until today.

But there are other factors too. It's utilitarian. It turns out that with modern science, especially in the last century or two, the ability to gain deeper understanding of the world has interacted critically with modern economic development, modern power. In fact, the course of science and the course of military endeavors is very close, way back to Archimedes. Archimedes was, after all, designing devices for military purposes. And military technology and science, their history closely interweaves in the modem period, particularly since the mid-nineteenth century. The sciences have actually begun to contribute materially to industrial development. So there are utilitarian purposes, but I wouldn't overexaggerate them. It's like the kind of result that led to freedom in other domains, like slavery, let's say. Or after a hundred and fifty years of American history, women were allowed to vote. Things like that. These are significant. Back to the point, especially after the great scientific revelations of the seventeenth century, it got to the point where you simply couldn't do science if you were subjected to the doctrinal controls that are quite effective outside the hard sciences. You can't do it. You try to be a physicist after Newton spinning off ideological fanaticism, and you're just out of the game. Progress was too much. It's striking.

You can see it right here in Cambridge. I've lived here almost all my adult life. There are two major academic institutions only a couple of miles apart. One of them is science and technology based, MIT. The other has sciences of course, but the tone of it is basically humanities and social sciences, Harvard. And the atmosphere is radically different. In fact, there is a funny problem in the natural sciences, an internal conflict. The goal, and in fact what you're being paid for, to put it crassly, why you're being given the opportunities, is to find out the truth about the world. And you can't do that under doctrinal constraints. So there's a tension. On the one hand it just has to be free, and it just has to encourage independent thought. On the other hand, people with power and authority want it to be constrained. That contradiction is much more striking in the natural sciences than it is in the social sciences or humanities. You can tell falsehoods forever there.

**But that implies that in the social sciences and economics and so on, to be crass, what they're being paid for is not to find the truth but something else.**

They are performing their role as long as they provide ideological services. To make it simple, take, say, modern economic theory, with its sort of free-market ideology. Planners in business and government are not going to waste their time following those rules. So the US has a steel industry because it radically violated those rules. It was able to recover its steel industry in the last ten years under allegedly free-market doctrine by barring all imports from abroad, by destroying labor unions so you could wipe down wages, and just a couple of days ago by slamming tariffs up to over 100 percent on foreign steel. That's planning. On the other hand, the free-market ideology is very useful. It's a weapon against the general population here because it's a weapon against social spending. It's a weapon against poor people abroad, saying, "You guys have to follow these rules." As long as the economists are providing what looks like an intellectual basis for this ideology, they're doing their job. You don't have to pay attention to them for actual planning. You can't do that with physics.

**How does it happen? Here we have students who finish undergraduate work and decide they want to be an economist. So they go to, let's say, Harvard or MIT or some other school in economics. Presumably when they come in they have some notion of doing something that's relevant to society, to making it a little better; something like that, at least a reasonable number of them. When they come out, they're either going to teach at some small community college or they've learned the correct lesson. But no one gets up in front of the class and says, "We will henceforth serve the interests of capital."**

It happens in a lot of ways. Let me tell you a story I once heard from a black civil rights activist who came up to Harvard Law School and was there for a while. This must have been twenty years ago. He once gave a talk and said that kids were coming into Harvard Law School with long hair and backpacks and social ideals and they were all going to go into public service, law, and change the world. That's the first year. He said around April the recruiters come for the summer jobs, the Wall Street firms. Get a cushy summer job and make a ton of money. So the students figure, "What the heck? I can put on a tie and jacket and shave for one day, because I need that money, and why shouldn't I have it?" So they put on a tie and a jacket for that one day and they get the job for the summer. Then they go off for the summer and when they come back in the fall, it's ties and jackets and obedience and a shift of ideology.

**Sometimes it takes two years.**

Sometimes it takes two years; that's overdrawing the point. But those factors are very influential. I've fought it all my life. It's extremely easy to be sucked into the dominant culture. It's very appealing. And the people don't look like bad people. You don't want to sit there and insult them. You try to be friends, and you are. You begin to conform, to adapt, to smooth off the harsher edges. Education at a place like Harvard is in fact largely geared to that, to a remarkable extent. I was a graduate student there. There was an organization called the Society of Fellows, which is a research outfit that selects a couple of people from all fields over the year. It was a remarkable opportunity to work. You had all the facilities of Harvard available and basically no responsibilities. Your only responsibilities were to show up for a dinner every Monday night, which was sort of modeled on the Oxford-Cambridge high table. You spent the evening at the dinner with a couple of senior faculty members and other distinguished people. The purpose of that was basically socialization. You had to learn how to drink port and how to have polite conversations without talking about serious topics, but of course indicating that you could talk about serious topics if you were so vulgar as to actually do it. There's a whole set of mannerisms. In those days you had to learn how to wear British clothes. That was the appropriate affectation.

**And it's rare for a person to do all that and not begin to rationalize and think, "This is really pretty good. Aren't I something for all this?" and to begin to be impressed.**

It kind of seeps in. They've had, for example, back in the early 1940s . . . in the 1930s of course there was pretty big labor strife and labor struggle, and it scared the daylights out of the business community because labor was actually winning the right to organize and even legislative victories. There were a lot of efforts to overcome this. Harvard played its role. It introduced a trade union program which brought in rising young people in the labor movement, the guy who looks like he's likely to be the local president next year. They're brought to Harvard, they sit in the business school and the dorms. They go through a socialization process. They're brought to share some of the values and an understanding of the elite. They're taught, "Our job is to work together. We all are together." There are two lines. One line, for the public, is, "We're all together. We're all cooperating, joint enterprise, harmony, and so on." Of course, meanwhile, business is fighting a vicious class struggle on the side, but that's in a different corner of the universe. That effort to socialize and integrate union activists, I've never measured its success, but I'm sure it was successful. It's pretty much the way what I experienced and saw a Harvard education. There's much less of that at MIT, naturally, for exactly the reason you said: They're not training the people who are going to rule.

It reminds me of 180 degrees opposite: when people started to become politicized in the early and mid-1960s, there was an intellectual component that was trying to understand society. There was a whole set of lifestyle acts, ranging from long hair to having a mattress on the floor to various other kinds of behavioral traits. Most parents were sophisticated enough to get much more upset about the lifestyle acts than about the ideas that were being phrased, because [those acts] had a tremendous tenacity. Once you had a community that had these lifestyle ways of behaving and ways of getting along and ways of identifying one another and being part of the same thing, you could escape the more mainstream behaviorisms far more easily. You could look at the accepted roles as being silly or false or whatever, and it was no longer so attractive. That has been absent since about 1970. I don't think the Left has had anything much to compete with the sort of general life definitions of the mainstream and the Right. So on the left you don't have a strong lifestyle and an identity to make it easy to ignore the seductions. What you have is ideals but no counteridentity. That's partly because the alternative lifestyle simply was commercialized and absorbed into the mainstream culture, selling clothes and that sort of thing.

**That was part of it. It was also partly because the alternative lifestyle was never the wonderful lifestyle it was cut out to be. Instead of defining something positively, it was defined as the opposite of what is. The opposite of something that's horrible isn't always so wonderful. So there were many components of the way we lived and acted in the late 1960s that were not well conceived as ways to live and act over a long period of time. They worked for a time, but over the longer haul they often just weren't very fulfilling.**

What you're saying is no doubt true. The thing has been commercialized and cheapened. Still, life's a lot easier than it was forty years ago. If I think back to those days, if I look at pictures from the early 1960s, I can hardly believe it, how disciplined everything was, how deep the authority structures were just in personal relations, the way you looked and talked when you went out with your friends. There's been very significant . . . I think [there were] very good changes as a result of what took place in the 1960s that in turn spread around the whole society. Maybe the spread of some of the gains meant that young dissidents couldn't identify themselves so easily, but it's in part because the society got better.

**But it's distracting and sort of disturbing. I mean, it's true, and when I talk to students I try to convey the difference between a time when everybody thought that every lawyer was honest and forthright and deserved obedience and so on and that doctors were out for nothing except to help humanity, that business people cared about consumers, and so on, to a time, now, when people know much more than that; to a time, now, when people are sort of passive and laid back. But then it's distracting that with those changes you don't have a parallel change in an organized and aware, self-conscious and critically aware left. On the one hand we do have a lot of left activists. But we don't have something that is a national Left.**

I agree with you, of course. But it seems to me what's happened, as I try to understand what's happened since the 1960s, is that there has been among the general population, excluding those who are considered responsible intellectuals, meaning the ones filling their tasks, excluding power structures and the intellectuals who serve their interests, for the general population, there has been something of almost a revolutionary change in moral values and cultural level and so on, and a great improvement. It has taken no institutional form at all. On the one hand, the ideological institutions are firmly in the hands of the extremely narrow liberal-to-reactionary spectrum, and very tightly controlled. There's no identifiable point of view or ways of thinking or by and large even journals outside them, very little. On the other hand, the general population has become extremely dissident and has absorbed many of the values that people were struggling for in the 1960s, and you can see it in just about every area.

**But the thing that seems to be missing is that then people thought that you could win a change.**

I think they did win a change.

**Yes, but it was in considerable part because they also believed they could, understood they could. But now people tend not to believe they can, and so have little incentive to try.**

I don't think they've recognized what changes are already achieved. If you take almost any area you think of, whether it's race or sex or military intervention, the environment, these are all areas of awareness and concern that didn't exist in the early 1960s. You didn't even think about them. You just submitted without even knowing that you were submitting. You just accepted. And people don't anymore. Take the original sin of American history: what happened to the native population? It's a remarkable fact that until the 1960s the culture simply couldn't come to terms with it. Not at all. When I grew up, I would go out with my friends and we'd play cowboys and Indians and shoot the Indians. Scholarship was the same. Until the 1960s, with very rare exceptions, academic scholarship was grossly falsifying the history, suppressing the reality of what happened. Even the number of people was radically falsified. As late as 1969, in one of the leading diplomatic histories of the United States, the author Thomas Bailey could write that after the Revolution "the colonists turned to the task of felling trees and Indians." Nobody could say that now. You couldn't even say that in a *Wall Street Journal* editorial. Those are really important changes.

**But somehow it's as if we snatched defeat from the jaws of victory. People have this perception of accomplishing nothing or very little and begin to burn out and to retain some of the values and commitments but begin to feel that you can no longer struggle for change because we're not succeeding. This is a common sentiment. It's certainly a common sentiment among people I know, not always voiced, I think, but there. Yet if you look objectively at the thing, like you're trying to do now, you see that if you don't have an outrageously inflated view of how fast change takes place, then you can understand that change has been dramatic. It isn't so obvious what the mechanism is that causes people to be so oblivious to their own effects.**

Partly it's that there's nothing in the official culture that's ever going to tell you you succeeded. It's always going to tell you that you failed. The official view of the 1960s is that it's a bunch of crazies running around burning down universities and making noise because they were hysterics or were afraid to go to Vietnam or something. That's what people hear. They may know in their lives and experience that that's not what happened, but they don't hear anybody say it unless they're in activist groups. That change is possible, that it has been won, is not the message that the system is pouring into you through television and radio and newspapers and books and histories and so on. It's sort of beating into your head another story. The other story is that you failed, and you should have failed, because you were just a bunch of crazies. And it's natural that the official culture should take that view. It does not want people to understand that you can make changes. That's the last thing it wants people to understand. So what the mainstream media conveys is that if there have been changes, it's because we, the elites, are so great that we carried through the changes.

But there's an element of truth in that, though perverse. Of course, short of a revolution any change that occurs is going to occur how? Immediately, because an elite makes a decision to enact a change. They're going to make the decision because of the pressures of social movements. But they are in a position to deny the influence of the movements and claim credit for themselves down the road a ways.

**But really, they bowed to pressures.**
That's right. When you read the histories, they don't talk about the pressures from social movements. Instead elites simply talk about their profound wisdom in taking this next step.

**We ended slavery because we were such great figures that we decided that we didn't like slavery.**
And the real cause of it is gone.

**Let's say the slave revolts.**
That's gone.

And sure, we saw that on a not-trivial scale in the last thirty years. So this combination of a kind of a, in my opinion, really close to revolutionary change in moral values and cultural level has gone on without any lasting institutional change. And the lack of institutional support for the changes in ideas and values allows the official culture to drive home its message, which is, "you guys are worthless and can't do anything, why don't you just shut up and go home?" And steadily they undermine the progress.

**I want to go into some of that when we talk about movements and what should happen. But let's just go back to this broad question of intellectuals. What about left intellectuals? If an intellectual is somebody**

**who spends time trying to understand, and a social intellectual tries to understand society, what's a left intellectual? Are there any?**
I've never been happy about words like "left" and "right," but let's use it in the conventional sense. One of the very few predictions in the social sciences that I know of that ever came true was one of Bakunin's over a century ago in which he talked about what the intellectuals were going to be like in modern industrial society. He predicted that they would fall into two categories: There would be the left intellectual. They would be the ones who would try to rise to power on the backs of mass popular movements, and if they could gain power they would then beat the people into submission.

**Leninism.**
Yes, what he was predicting was Leninism. And if the intellectuals find that they can't do that, or that it is too dangerous or costly, they'll be the servants of what we would nowadays call state capitalism. He didn't use the term. Either of the two intellectuals, he said, will be "beating the people with the people's stick." That is, they will still be presenting themselves as representatives of the people, so they'll hold the people's stick, but they'll be beating the people with it. He didn't go on with this, but I think that his analysis has turned out to be true. And it follows from his analysis that it would likely be extremely easy to shift from one position to the other. It's extremely easy, that is, to undergo what nowadays is called the "God-that-failed" syndrome. You start off as basically a Leninist, someone who is going to be part of the Red bureaucracy. You see later that power doesn't lie that way, and you very quickly become an ideologist of the Right and you devote your life to exposing the sins of your former comrades who haven't seen the light and haven't shifted to where power really is. In fact, we're seeing it right now in the Soviet Union. The same guys who were Communist thugs, Stalinist thugs, two years back are now running banks and enthusiastic free marketeers and praising Americans.

**It doesn't take a long indoctrination period to learn the new style.**
And this has been going on for forty years. It's become a kind of a joke. Where does that leave what you might call "honest intellectuals?" They're usually outside the system, for good reasons. There is no reason to expect institutions of power and domination to tolerate people trying to undermine them. Quite the opposite. So therefore you quite typically find the honest and serious intellectuals, people who are committed to, I think,

enlightenment values, values of truth, freedom, liberty, and justice, there would be major efforts made to marginalize them.

**Who are they?**
All the people who have done anything that's . . .

**Who, which people, groups?**
Take, say, the SNCC [Student Nonviolent Coordinating Committee] activists. They were serious intellectuals. They made a big change in the world. The people of your generation, who did the work that led to the changes we spoke of earlier . . . work that didn't just mean running around the streets waving signs. It also meant thinking about things and figuring out what the problems were. Those people made a change. A certain number of them did filter their way into the institutions. For example, if you take universities or newspapers or television today, you usually find people in there, almost always, who have been through those experiences and have remained true to them. They've got to adapt their behavior in various ways to get by, but many of them do it very self-consciously, very honestly and even very constructively. So there's a kind of an honest intelligentsia if you like, meaning not serving power, either as Red bureaucracy or as state capitalist, commissar equivalents. Such people exist, sometimes in the institutions, but most of the time out of them, for almost trivial reasons. The institutions are simply not going to welcome serious critics. They're constructed in such a way as to make it difficult or impossible for people who are going to undermine those institutions to survive. How could it be otherwise? It's just like you're not going to find a militant labor activist as chair of the board of General Electric. How could it be?

**It seems straightforward to me as well. But we come to the question, are there some left intellectuals who rise to a position of relative prominence, so they're visible. SNCC activists are anonymous, in a sense, socially anonymous.**
They're marginalized, but they're important. Some of them are still around, doing important things.

**But in a sense it's an activist group who is not highlighted and made publicly visible. And some leaders might be.**
Like Rosa Luxemburg, say, who got killed.

**Right. So there's a figure in history who we could say, "She's one of the people who I would pick . . ."**
She was murdered. That's the point.

**Typical. This raises the question, Can we only find dead . . . ?**
No. First of all, if you look back through history . . .

**Let's look now.**
Now? You find people all over. It's claimed now that there's less of a left intelligentsia than there was thirty years ago. I don't believe a word of it. Take a look at the people who they're calling the Left, the big thinkers of the 1950s. Who were they? They were intelligent people. Ed Wilson is an intelligent person, but a left intellectual? Mary McCarthy? A smart person who wrote some nice novels but not a left intellectual. In fact, now you have much more serious activists in many more places.

I travel all the time and give talks all over the place. I've been amazed to go to places throughout the 1980s . . . take, say, the Central America solidarity movement, which is a pretty dramatic development. I don't think there's been anything like it in history. I'd go to a church in Kansas or a town in Montana or Wyoming or Anchorage, Alaska, and find people who knew more about Latin America, certainly, than the CIA, which is not hard, but people in academic departments who've thought about it, who understood things about American policy. I can't even tell you their names. There are too many of them. Also, I'm not even sure that the word "left" is the right word for them. A lot of them were probably Christian conservatives, but they were very radical people in my view. Intellectuals who understood and did a lot. They created a popular movement which not only protested US atrocities but actually engaged themselves in the lives of the victims. In the 1960s nobody ever dreamt of going off to a Vietnamese village because maybe a white face in the village would limit the capacity of the marauders to kill and destroy. That wasn't even an idea in your head. In fact, nobody even went to try to report the war from the side of the victims. It was unheard of, save for a few "crazies." But in the 1980s it was common. And the people who were doing that are serious left intellectuals, in my view.

**So if a person comes along and says the left intellectual community is gutted, there's very little of it, what they must in fact be saying is**

something like—"the number of people who call themselves leftist and who are visibly notable is small." Which, of course, in your analysis may well be an indication that there a growing left intellectual community which is, of course, being isolated and not labeled anything publicly and not given any public visibility.

That's right. What will be labeled "left" and given publicity is something ugly enough that people can be rallied to oppose it. So Stalinism, for example. Books will come out, and are coming out, about the left intellectuals in France who were Stalinists. And look at the awful things they did. That kind of left intelligentsia is allowed to have publicity and prominence. They give them as much prominence as they can.

**It's useful.**

But if by "Left" you mean people who are struggling for peace and justice and freedom and human rights and so on, and for social change and elimination of authority structures, whether it's personal life or institutions or whatever, if that's what the Left is, there are more of them around than I remember in my lifetime.

**In coming to this kind of perception of the thing, you have a real advantage, you personally, relatively speaking. You personally, as compared to one of those individuals, do have a lot of the visibility and a lot of the access that somebody might attribute as the critical ingredient needed to impact on a wide audience in our society. These other people feel isolated. They feel relatively uninfluential or unable to express their opinions to a wider audience.**

Visibility, that's putting the cart before the horse. The reason I have visibility is because there are a lot of people around, a lot of groups around, who come and ask me to speak or because people ask me to write. I don't have visibility in the mainstream institutions.

**But there has to be a distinction between you and those people you mentioned in Omaha or Anchorage or wherever who may know more than you, or at least a lot, about Central America and who are never asked to speak.**

We pick different ways of living our lives. In the early 1960s I was an MIT professor. But when I started giving talks about the war or organizing tax resistance or getting involved in the foundation of RESIST, national resistance support groups, or being faculty advisor for the Rosa Luxemburg SDS at MIT, I didn't have any visibility. There are choices to be made. Some of my close friends who have the same status and chance for visibility that I had actually picked a different way and devoted their lives to organizing and activism. Louis Kampf and I are old friends. We taught courses together for years at MIT, courses which you took years ago. We just went different ways. He devoted himself primarily to real activism and organizing and keeping groups and journals functioning and so on. I tried that and I wasn't any good at it. I found that I was much better at other things, and that there seemed to be a demand for the other things, so I just went that way. That ends up in me being visible. He's visible in other circles than the ones that I'm visible in. But those are just different ways of reacting to the same sorts of problems, depending on your personality and your particular abilities and the kinds of things you can do and the kinds of things you can't do and so on and so forth. The visibility is a surface phenomenon. Visibility is the result of the existence of an active, lively Left. If what I've been talking about as the Left were to disappear, I would no longer be visible.

**As a political commentator.**
Yes, I could still appear in linguistics and philosophy meetings, but I would certainly not be visible as a political commentator, because there would be nowhere for me to open my mouth except to my friends. It would be back to the early 1960s, when I could talk to people in the living room. The reason that it has changed is because there are opportunities that in fact call for this kind of participation, so that makes people look visible. We mentioned SNCC before. Why did Martin Luther King become visible? Because there were SNCC workers down in the South, and he could appear and serve a role for them.

**It seems to me there is a positive and negative side to that. The positive side you've described: there's a political context and it draws people in different ways and people participate. But the negative side seems to me to be, you gave the examples of Martin Luther King and yourself. There's a need for a particular visible organizer or a particular visible speaker and proselytizer of information, a presenter of information. But once those slots are filled, then there's a tendency for people to cling to the individuals who are filling those slots. For a long period of**

time, depending on a number of factors, the number of slots might not broaden out. Nowadays if a group in Cleveland or in San Francisco or wherever wants an antiwar speaker during the Gulf crisis or wants a speaker about foreign policy, very few names pop into mind. Whereas I think you're right, there is a much larger circuit of people, especially if they had the experience of engaging in those activities, who could fill the bill. That seems to me to be not so positive a dynamic.

It's not. It's hard to break through. There are people who we know in fact who are highly qualified to do lots of things and are eager to do it but sort of can't pass over that barrier. I don't know exactly what the reason for that is, frankly, because all of us had to pass over that barrier at some point. Part of the reason is that there haven't been a lot of people available. Take, say, the last ten years, when there's been a lot of activism, a lot of it having to do with Latin America. There just haven't been a lot of people around who were willing to go and give talks. There are plenty of people who are willing to write articles on postmodernism and the Left or whatever but not many who are willing to go to a town somewhere and give a talk at a meeting. We can name them.

**Or we can name the ones we know but it may well be there are a good many more and we can't name them. That's the problem.**

There are a good many more who would be highly qualified and maybe even would like to do it. The question we're asking is "How come they don't?" and I don't know what the answer is. First of all, I don't think it's all that hard. Take, say, people who weren't known very well, like Holly Sklar, who probably wasn't known fifteen years ago. She got plenty of invitations all over the place. She became visible. There are others like her. Take my friend Norman Finkelstein on the Middle East. He can get plenty of invitations to speak. He's been totally shut out of the institutions, but he's visible if he wants. It can be done. It's not so simple.

**It's somewhat difficult. I do think that there's a dynamic there that closes it off.**

The bad dynamic, what you're pointing to, is the "star story. It's standard when a popular movement takes off for people to show up and say, "Okay, I'm your leader." A Eugene McCarthy type, say. Here's a big popular movement. "Fine. I'm your leader. Give me power. If you can't give me power I'll go home and write poetry and talk about baseball. And if you can give me power then I become your leader and now you look up to me and you go home and put the power in my hand." That's a familiar dynamic, and Bakunin's Red bureaucracy, no matter what its politics are. It could be right-wing, it could be left-wing. But there's a better dynamic, which is that the popular movements continue and strengthen, and where there are people around who, for whatever reason or quirk or privilege or whatever it may be, can contribute to them by intellectual activity, they do a part of it. That's all. They're not stars. They're not leaders. They're just contributing in the way that they know how to contribute. That would be a better structure. But it can tend to degenerate into this other very quickly, especially in a culture which is reinforcing their worst tendencies by trying to create an imagery of leadership and stars and heroes and so on.

**Suppose somebody could convince you, at the level of your belief in most things, that it's impossible to change the country. Suppose they convinced you that the basic institutional structure that we have now is going to be in place for the next two hundred years, adapted sure, but the basic structures as they are. Would you behave any differently?**
Zero.

**You would behave exactly the same way**
The same way. In fact, you don't even have to make it hypothetical. When I got seriously involved in anti–Vietnam War activities, I was 100 percent convinced that absolutely nothing could be done, and there was plenty of reason to believe that. I was giving plenty of talks, but they were usually in living rooms to a group of neighbors that somebody would get together. They were usually pretty hostile. Or in a church where there would be four people including some guy who wandered in because he didn't know what to do, and two people who wanted to kill you, and the organizer. Into 1965 and 1966, if we wanted to have at MIT an antiwar meeting, we would have to find six topics. Let's talk about Venezuela, Iran, Vietnam, and the price of bread, and maybe we can get an audience that will outnumber the organizers. And that went on for a long time. As you well remember, it was impossible to have a public meeting in Boston without it being smashed up. It looked impossible.

**If you thought this was going to continue forever, you would still do it. I think it would be useful to explain why.**

A number of quite simple reasons. For one thing, if somebody convinced me, it would be because I'm totally irrational. There's no way you could convince anybody of such things rationally. We cannot predict the weather two weeks ahead, and we even understand why we can't.

**It's a hypothetical question. It gets to motivations. Obviously neither one of us believe it, and neither one of us believe you could prove it. You couldn't convince anybody rational of it.**
You couldn't say anything convincing about it.

**Nevertheless, supposing because a great many people not understanding that point, do feel this way or tend to feel this way sometimes and get depressed at moments. The question is, in any event, what gets you up each morning to do the things that you do. Is it that you think in terms of winning a little ways down the road, or is it something else?**
It's hard to introspect, but to the extent that I introspect about it, it's because you basically have two choices. One choice is to assume the worst, and then you can be guaranteed that it will happen. The other is to assume that there is hope for change, and then it's possible that by acting you will help effect change. So you've got two choices. One guarantees that the worst will happen. The other leaves open the possibility that things might be better. Given those two choices, a rational person doesn't hesitate.

I used to think about this back when I was becoming political, in the mid-1960s. I played the hypothetical game a little more fairly than I think you are right now. I said to myself, "Okay, suppose it's haves and have-nots. Not very many haves, a whole lot of have-nots. Forever. Which side do you want to be on?" And it's not an easy question. At the time it was trivial. In the 1960s, that was an easy question to answer. You wanted to be on the side of the have-nots regardless of prospects. I think this had a lot to do with lifestyle and values and who you identify with. The other stuff, being a have, just wasn't attractive. Now I think it's a much harder question.

But that's one kind of motivation that people can have for being radical. The other kind of motivation that people can have for being radical is the inclination that you're going to win tomorrow or in your lifetime or in a reasonable span of time. It seems like the first motivation breeds a different kind of person in some sense than the second. They're called purists, morally motivated, ethically motivated, and scorned a bit by some of the other types, with some reason. Because—and this was the other thing that I began to realize early on—trying to make social change isn't like trying to play socialist basketball. In working for social change, the score counts. It doesn't do to play well or congenially but lose. The combination of both of those motivations—scorning being a have but also seriously wanting to win—in one person seems to me to be rather difficult.

You mentioned two possibilities. One is a description of your own group's experience in the 1960s. You didn't expect to win a huge victory tomorrow. Some people expected we'll go out and strike at Columbia. . . . And everybody will love each other and that's the end of power. We both know perfectly well that plenty of people believed that. There were other people who recognized it was going to be a long struggle but who were joining with like-minded people who shared their cultural values and their lifestyle and everything else. There's also a third type. You've got me; I was not part of the cultural scene. I certainly didn't expect a quick victory. I kept my old-fashioned bourgeois lifestyle, and I haven't changed it to this day. And there are people like that too. If we go on, there are many more types of people. People can come in a lot of varieties. But it seems to me that it always comes down to the individual decision: What am I going to do? Here are my options. Of course, my personal options are broader than those of most other people, because I happen to be very privileged, but everybody's got some option. You ask yourself, "Will I not use them at all? In which case I can be sure that suffering will continue and oppression will continue and discrimination will continue and get worse. Or will I use whatever options I have, try to work with others to change things? In which case things may get better." It seems to me that ultimately that's what things come down to, no matter who we are. And given those choices, a decent person is only going to go one way. That's exactly why society and the official culture doesn't want you to understand that you have those choices.

**Is that true that a decent person's only going to go one way? I'm remembering a friend of mine who was an organizer in the 1960s. We went through the antiwar movement. Then came a little bit further along and there was a trend toward doing community organizing, moving into a neighborhood, trying to organize people in that neighborhood.**

This individual was going to move into a neighborhood in Dorchester, in Boston, a working-class area, and try and do organizing. He finally decided not to do it and somewhat later went back to graduate school and then became a psychiatrist and now, I'm sure, has progressive values at some level—I haven't seen him in years and years—but is certainly not involved in any significant way in political activity. The choice that he made was a very self-conscious one. He looked around him and said, "The impact that I personally am going to have is so small because I'm not so-and-so or so-and-so." He'd name some other people who had prospects of maybe in his eyes having more impact, because of whatever set of factors. "So it simply isn't worth giving up what I think I'm giving up." I don't know who you mean, but I know plenty of people like that. That person now, let's say he's a rich psychiatrist somewhere . . .

**He's probably reasonably well-off.**
He's got a lot of options. For example, he's got money.

**This is like a person going to Harvard Law School. The probability that he'll do something good with his income after the years of earning it.**
I agree. But he's simply deciding at some point not to face the options. He's always got them. He may decide, "Look, I can't make enough of a change myself because I'm not good at it or whatever, so I'm just going to do what I like and enrich myself." But having done so, you still have plenty of options available. In fact, movement groups have existed in part because people who were doing other things were willing to fund them. You can go way beyond that, of course, and still live your elegant lifestyle and do the work you want. We know people who have divided their lives that way. Of course it's extremely easy to say, "The heck with it. I'm just going to adapt myself to the structures of power and authority and do the best I can within them." Sure, you can do that. But that's not acting like a decent person. You can walk down the street and be hungry. You see a kid eating an ice cream cone, notice there's no cop around, and take the ice cream cone from him because you're bigger, and walk away. You can do that. Probably there are people who do. We call them "pathological." On the other hand, if they do it within existing social structures we call them "normal." But it's just as pathological. It's just the pathology of the general society. And people, again, always have choices. We're free people. You can decide to accept that pathology, but then do it honestly, at least, if you

have that grain of honesty to say, "I'm going to honestly be pathological." Or else try to break out of it somehow.

But for a lot of people I think it appears that there's an all-or-nothing choice. It appears that there's the choice of being normal—pathological as you describe, but a normal member of society with its normal benefits and costs and so on, but at least a reasonably average or perhaps elite existence that's accepted. Then there seems to be another "all" choice, to be a raging revolutionary. It's so hard for many people even just to take a leaflet from a protester or donate at a relatively low level that means nothing financially—less money than they're going to spend on dinner on Friday night when they go out—or to do some other materially trivial act. The reason this is hard seems to be that there's a really powerful psychological effect. The effect seems to me to be that at some level people know that to dissent is right, and at some level people know that to do it somewhat leads to doing it still more, so they defensively close the door right at the beginning. They have a very hard time finding a place in that span of possible involvement that allows them to be a functioning human being with a degree of fulfillment in society and also lets them contribute to dramatically changing society.

You're right. Just giving your contribution of one hundred dollars to the Central America support center or whatever is a statement that you know that that's the right thing to do. Once you've stated it's the right thing to do, "how come I'm only doing this limited thing since I could do a million times more?" It's easier to say, "I'm not going to face that problem at all. I'm just going to forget it entirely." But that's like stealing the ice cream cone from the kid.

But it says something to the Left or to movements and organizers. It is at some level unreasonable to think that in the absence of hope or in the presence only of small hope and not a clear understanding of how one's going to make progress, that people are going to shift all the way from being average, normal, everyday folks of one type or another over to being political revolutionaries, people who see things in political terms. If there's no set of choices in the middle that are comfortable and that allow people to operate and to retain some of their lifestyle, then it's not likely that too many are going to do anything. You almost have to be religious to make the jump.

But the reality is there's a whole range of choices in the middle.

**But people don't see them.**
And all of us have made them. None of us are saints, at least I'm not. I haven't given up my house and car, and I don't live in a hovel. I don't spend twenty-four hours a day working for the benefit of the human race or anything like that. I don't even come close. I spend an awful lot of my time and energy . . .

**And you don't feel guilty about whatever else is it that you're doing, linguistics or . . .**
That's not so clear. But at least I certainly devote an awful lot of my energy and activity to things that I just enjoy, like scientific work. I just like it. I do it out of pleasure. And everybody else I know . . .

**Do you fool yourself into believing that doing that increases your effectiveness as a political person?**
No, that's ridiculous. It has no effect on it. And I don't do it for that reason. I like it. I mean, I can make up a story . . .

**I think people have a hard time doing this. And that's why a lot of people do nothing politically dissident.**
That's true, but if we were to go back to that small class of people who are visible, every one of them does this. Every single one.

**Almost by definition.**
Because you're not going to be effective as a political activist unless you have a satisfying life. There may be people who are really saints. I've never heard of one.

**By definition they're not saints, because they're getting so much satisfaction out of the political activity, they're not saintly at it.**
Not from the political activity. It may be that the political activities themselves are so gratifying that's all you want to do, so you throw yourself into that. That's a perfectly fine thing to be. It's just that most people have other interests. They want to listen to music. They want to take a walk by the ocean. Any human being is too rich and complex to be just satisfied with these things. You have to hit some kind of a balance. The choices are all there. And I think you've identified precisely why it's psychologically

difficult for people to recognize that choices are there. Because once you recognize that the choices are there, you're always going to be faced with the question, "Why am I not doing more?" But that's the reality of life. If you're honest, you're always going to be faced with those questions. And there's plenty to do. In fact, if you look back over the last period, there's a lot of successes to point to. It's amazing how many successes there are if you really think about it.

Take something which very few people have been interested in. Take the issue of East Timor, the massacre. I got involved in that about fifteen years ago. People didn't even want to hear about it. Things finally got to the point where the US Congress barred military aid to Indonesia. That's a tremendous change. You could save hundreds of thousands of lives that way. How many people can look back and say, "Look, I helped save hundreds of thousands of lives?" And that's one tiny issue.

**I'm inclined to think that most of the people who are involved in that effort, instead of feeling elated or feeling at least a degree of satisfaction over their accomplishment, rather probably view it as a horrendously long campaign with very little achieved. It's like saying the glass is half-empty instead of half-full, except we see it empty even when it's almost full.**

Suppose you're on your deathbed. How many people can look back and say, I've contributed to helping . . . just one person not get killed?

**I'm not disagreeing with you. I think you're right, clearly. But there's something that causes people, maybe something about our culture, to not see it.**

I'm not so convinced of this. The 1960s movements, roughly speaking, were almost overwhelmingly young people. Young people have a notoriously short perspective. It's part of being twenty years old. You don't think what's going to happen tomorrow. I've seen it around students, around children, even. I remember myself. You don't think what's life going to be like twenty years from now. Your perspective is short. The fact that it was a youth movement dominantly had good and bad aspects. One bad aspect was this sense that if we don't achieve gains quickly we might as well quit. But of course that's not the way changes come. The struggle against slavery, let's say, went on forever. The struggle for women's rights has been going on for a century. The effort to overcome wage slavery has been going on since the beginning of the Industrial Revolution, and we haven't advanced an inch. In fact, we are worse off than a hundred years ago in terms of understanding the issues. Well, okay, you just keep struggling.

**Let's go back to one of the things that you mentioned when you were talking about academics, what role they play, what they're doing, and what their time goes to. You brought up briefly in passing postmodernism and these various other . . . you can either call them insightful forays into knowledge or fads. I know, and probably most people listening know, at least somewhat, about your reaction to it. But let's go over it anyway. Where does it come from? Why does a person who has a tremendous amount of educational background, knowledge, experience, and time spend it on something akin to astrology?**
I don't want to overgeneralize. I think there is important and insightful work done in those frameworks. I find it really hard to figure out because I've got to labor to try to tease the simple, interesting points out. But there are things there. I think we're making progress there. But I think there's a point that's much more general. The fact is, it's extremely hard to have good ideas. There are very few of them around. If you're in the sciences, you know you can sometimes come up with something pretty startling, usually something that's small in comparison with what's known, and you're really excited about it. Outside the natural sciences it's extremely hard to do even that. There just isn't that much that's complicated that's at all understood outside of pretty much the core natural sciences. Everything else is either too hard for us to understand or pretty easy.

**So suppose you're making $50,000 a year as an academic in that field?**
You've got to have a reason for your existence. The result is that simple ideas are dressed up in extremely complex terminology and frameworks. In part it's just careerism, or maybe an effort to build self-respect. Take, say, what's called "literary theory." I don't think there's any such thing as literary theory, any more than there's cultural theory.

**And obviously you can read a book and talk about it.**
Yeah, if you're reading books and talking about them and getting people to . . .

**You could be very good at that.**

You could be terrific at it. Take, say, Edmund Wilson. He's terrific at it. But he doesn't have a literary theory. On the other hand, if you want to be in the same room with that physicist over there who's talking about quarks, you better have a complicated theory, too, that nobody can understand. He has a theory that nobody can understand, so why shouldn't I have a theory that nobody can understand?

**The interesting thing is that the physicist will write about that theory in a popular book and explain it without a whole lot of rigmarole. It won't all be explained, but a great deal of it will be. A physicist of the modern period could write a book that you could give to your twelve-year-old kid and she'll understand it and learn something from it. In fact, I see it myself all the time. What's the reason why literary theorists can't do that? Is it because there's nothing there?**
That's my assumption. Either there's something there that's so deep that it's a kind of qualitative change in human intelligence, or there isn't a lot there. And it's not just literary theory. If somebody came along with a theory of history, it would be the same. "Theory" would be a sort of truism. Maybe "smart ideas." Somebody could have smart ideas and say, "Why don't you look at class struggle? It's interesting." Or, "Why don't you look at economic factors lying behind the Constitution?" Pick your topic. Those are interesting smart ideas. But you can say them in monosyllables. And it's rare outside the natural sciences to find things that can't be said in monosyllables. There are interesting, simple ideas. They're often hard to come up with, and they're often extremely hard to work out. Like you want to try to understand what actually happened, say, in the modern industrial economy and how it developed the way it is. That can take a lot of work. But there isn't going to be anything too complex to talk about. The theory will be extremely thin, if by "theory" we mean something with principles which are not obvious when you look at them from which you can deduce surprising consequences, check out the consequences, and then confirm the principles. You're not going to find anything like that.

**So we can imagine two libraries: a library of literary theory books, postmodernism, and so on; and another library with Marxist-Leninist books in essentially the same building.**
I don't understand that either. I read all kinds of things that talk about dialectical materialism. I haven't the foggiest idea what it is.

**It's a word like "postmodernism."**
To me at least, yes. I've said this occasionally in interviews and I get long letters back from people saying, "You don't understand. Here's what dialecticalism is."

**And it's incomprehensible again.**
Either it's incomprehensible or it's true but totally obvious. People can be tone-deaf too; they can't hear music. So maybe I'm tone-deaf about this stuff or something. Everything I find in these fields either seems to be interesting but pretty obvious, once you see it—maybe you didn't see it, somebody has to point it out to you, but once you see it, it's obvious—or else the subject is just incomprehensible. In other fields it's quite different. If I pick up the latest issue of *Physics Review*, I'm not going to understand one word. But there's two differences: First of all, I know perfectly well what I would have to do to get to understand. And in some areas I've done it, although I'm not particularly good at it. But I can do it. The other thing is what you said before: I could ask you to tell me what this is about. I can go to some guy in the physics department and say, "Tell me, why is everybody excited about this stuff?" And they can tell it in a way which I can understand and adapt it to my level of understanding and also tell me how to go on if I want to. In these other areas, say, dialectical materialism or postmodern literary theory, there's just no way to do either of those things, which leads me to only two conclusions: Either I'm missing a gene, like tone deafness, which is conceivable, or it's a way of disguising maybe interesting ideas in an incomprehensible framework for reasons which ultimately turn out to be careerist. I don't want to criticize the people for being careerists. It's hard to live in this world, and you want to have self-respect. That's understandable and justifiable. And it turns out to be true that in most domains if there are hard things to understand, they're way beyond us.

**Another trend in thinking or in how people approach society and try and understand it is the approach that's called "conspiracy theory," which we've both encountered. It has gained a great deal of popularity, particularly on the West Coast. I wonder not so much in the specific instance of, say, JFK or other conspiracies that are discussed but more broadly in terms of what's the most useful or effective way to understand what's going on in society and interact with it? Is there something**

about conspiracy theory compared to, what, an approach emphasizing institutions and their implications? That's an obstacle that represents a hindrance on understanding the world to change it?

We want to find out the truth about the way things work. There are doubtless cases in which people get together; in fact, every example we find of planning decisions is a case where people got together and tried to figure something out and used their power or the power that they could draw from to try to achieve a result. If you like, that's a conspiracy. So with that definition everything that happens is a conspiracy. So if the board of General Motors gets together and decides what kind of Chrysler, Ford, something, to produce next year, that's a conspiracy. Every business decision, every editorial decision . . .

**Ultimately made by people.**

If my department gets together and decides who to appoint next year, okay, it's a conspiracy. That's not interesting. Obviously, all decisions involve people. If the word "conspiracy" is to have any sensible meaning, the question becomes whether there are groupings well outside the structure of the major institutions that go around them, hijack them, undermine them, and pursue other courses without an institutional base.

**So that would be the notion of conspiracy theory. Things happen because these groups exist and are outside the normal structures of society.**

Because these groups or subgroups act outside of the structure of institutional power, they are special, and we call them conspiracies. But as I look over history, I don't find much of that. There are some cases, like a group of Nazi generals who thought of assassinating Hitler. That's a conspiracy. But things like that are real blips on the screen, as far as I can see.

**Supposing there's some number of them, what do you gain from spending a lot of time trying to unearth them and uncover them and understand them?**

If people want to study the group of generals who decided that it was time to get rid of Hitler, that's a fine topic for a monograph, or maybe somebody will write a thesis on it, but we're not going to learn anything about the world from it. That will show how the people acted in particular circumstances. Fine.

**You say we're not going to learn anything about the world from it. That's true almost by definition. The whole idea is that these people act, in a sense, outside the normal functioning of the world, so studying them teaches us about them but not about typical and recurring patterns in history.**

They were acting outside because of unusual circumstances, exactly. And what's more, it's only a shade away from the board of Directors of General Motors sitting down in their executive suite and making their regular decisions. It's just a little bit away from that because they happened to depart somewhat from the major power structures. But we're not learning much about how the world works, in fact, nothing that generalizes to the next case. It's going to be historically contingent and specific. If you look at modern American history, where these issues have flourished, I think such cases are notable by their absence. At least as I read the record, it almost never happens. Occasionally you'll find something, like, say, the Reaganites with their off-the-shelf subversive and terrorist activities. But that's kind of a fringe operation. Probably the reason it got smashed pretty quickly is because the institutions are too powerful to tolerate it. Take, say, the CIA, which is considered the source of lots of conspiracies. We have a ton of information about them, and as I read the information, they're pretty loyal bureaucrats and do what they're told. As far as the Pentagon goes, they'll push their interests, and the services will push their interests, but in pretty transparent ways.

**So this is systemic, not conspiratorial. You have two arguments: One is, even if it exists, even if there are occasional or even frequent conspiracies, examining them is not going to teach us about that event. Not much about history or the way things work. The next claim is, well, there aren't even that many in the first place.**

What they usually are is what you'd find in a big corporation, a faculty, or any other structure you're in.

**You think it's generally a normal outgrowth of the operations of an institution.**

An institution has a certain structure of power. It has certain resources. It has an authority structure. It fits into the general society in certain ways, and if it tried to break out of those ways it would be undermined and destroyed. If General Motors decided to become a benevolent organization and produce good cars at the cheapest rates with the best working conditions, they'd be out of business tomorrow. Somebody who isn't doing it would undermine them. There are reasons why institutions operate the way they do within a bigger framework. Suppose, say, Bill Clinton, in a dream, was really going to behave like the British Labour Party thinks he is, namely the revolutionary who is going to bring about a social revolution. In one minute, bond prices would start to decline slightly. The interest rate would go up. The economy would start to collapse, and that's the end of that program. There are frameworks within which things happen.

**That's because he would be operating as an isolated individual with no power base just because he wants to, perhaps with a few allies, a conspiracy running against the grain, and getting nowhere.**
Exactly. And the people who have the power would say, "I don't like that, so I'll pull my money out of Treasury securities and put it somewhere else." And it goes down and you've got a response. In fact, if he doesn't understand it, he could have read a front-page article in the *Wall Street Journal* a couple of weeks ago explaining it in simple words, just in case anybody got any ideas. But you don't have to say it. Everybody understands it. We have tremendous concentrations of power throughout the society in the economy and the political system and the ideological system. They're all very interlinked in all kinds of ways, but the degree of power and authority and domination is extraordinary. If any renegade group tried to break out of that, they would quickly be in trouble and cut off. You can see it happening right at the top. Take, say, Nixon and Watergate. Watergate was just a triviality. In terms of the horrifying actions that the government carried out, Watergate isn't even worth laughing about. It was a tea party. It's kind of interesting to see what kind of issues were raised.

**A tea party except for one thing, which is that it was aimed at elites.**
It was aimed at elites. He broke out of the normal workings of power. He called Thomas Watson of IBM a bad name. He tried to undermine the Democratic Party, which is half of the business power in the country. Sure, he was called on the carpet and tossed out in three seconds. Not because he had violated some moral code. Essentially he was not attacked for the atrocities that he carried out. The FBI killed Fred Hampton during his administration, a straight Gestapo-style killing. That never came up at

Watergate. Take the dramatic bombing of Cambodia, this thing called the secret bombing of Cambodia, which was "secret" because the press didn't talk about what they knew. They killed probably a couple hundred thousand people. They devastated a peasant society. It came up, but only in one respect: Did he tell Congress about it? In other words, were people with power granted their prerogatives? That's the only issue that came up. You can see what happens when somebody even marginally breaks out of the system. They're quickly put back in their box, because they're servants. Real power lies elsewhere.

**And even there, it's not individuals. General Motors is an institution and the people who run it don't have that much power either.**
The head of IBM just got tossed out. Why? They didn't have enough profit last year. You either do your job or you're out. Power lies elsewhere. When the American corporate system decided the Vietnam War wasn't worth it for them anymore, they had gotten what they were going to get, they basically told Johnson to go back to Texas. He was fired. He was told, "You're not going to run. Pull out." Within a system that works like this, it would be pretty remarkable if there were anything remotely like what the various conspiracy theories conjure up. When you look at them, they just collapse, not surprisingly.

**With perhaps one exception: King's assassination.**
It's interesting. That's the one case where we can imagine pretty good reasons why somebody would want to kill him. I would not be in the least surprised if there was a real conspiracy behind that one, and probably a high-level one.

**Assuming it was Hoover; then, the mechanism is there, the means are there, everything is available. Nobody would be upset in the government.**
I don't think there's been a lot of inquiry into that one. If there has I'm not aware of it. But that's the one very plausible case. You're absolutely right. In the case of the one everybody's excited about, Kennedy, nobody has ever come up with a plausible reason.

**It's an interesting question: Why do you think, when you hear these people who believe in the efficacy of looking at conspiracy and trying to understand it, the amount of energy that goes into the Kennedy case**

**almost can't even be measured, it's off the scale, but the amount of energy that goes into the King case is relatively small.**

It's a pretty dramatic contrast, because the case of the King one is prima facie very plausible. The case of the Kennedy one is prima facie extremely implausible. So it is a question you want to ask.

**Perhaps if you have a conspiracy approach to things, the more implausible it is, the more outside of the normal grain it is, the more of a conspiracy it is, the more attractive it is to you. I don't know.**

There are things, in a way, conspiring to make the Kennedy case an attractive topic. One is just the glitter of Camelot. The Kennedy administration was in many ways similar to the Reagan administration in power.

**The glitter of Camelot is specks of blood.**

But the point is that the Kennedy administration did one smart thing: They buttered up the intellectual class, as compared with the Reaganites, who just treated them with contempt. The result was they got a terrific image. They gave an appearance of sharing power that was never real to the kind of people who write books and articles and make movies and that sort of thing. The result is that Camelot had a beautiful image, lovely imagery, and there's been great efforts to maintain that image. Somehow they succeeded in getting a lot of people to believe it. You can go to the South, to a poor, rural, black area, and you'll find pictures of Kennedy. In fact, Kennedy's role in the civil rights movement was not pretty. But somehow the imagery succeeded, even if the reality wasn't there. And it's certainly true that a lot of things have gone wrong in the last twenty, twenty-five years. Plenty of things have gone wrong, for all sorts of totally independent reasons, which one can talk about. The civil rights movement made great achievements but never lived up to the hopes that many people had invested in it. The antiwar movement made achievements, but it didn't end war. Real wages have been declining for twenty years. A lot of things have been happening that aren't pretty. It's easy to fall into the belief that we had a hero and we had a wonderful country and we had this guy who was going to lead us to a better future. We had the Messiah, they shot him down, and ever since then everything's been illegitimate.

**I remember when I was organizing in the 1960s and also since, though it is harder to elicit when less seems to be at stake, I would frequently**

encounter a view behind people's reticence to act or to become part of political movements. The view was basically that human nature is corrupt, egotistical, self-centered, antisocial, and that as a result of that, society would always be haves and have-nots, oppressors and oppressed, hierarchical and so on. I'd often find that in organizing you could get agreement on the inhumanity of a particular system or the illegality or injustice of, say, the war or some set of policies, more recently, but that people would refrain from becoming active around it because of a sense of hopelessness having to do with this view of human nature. It may have been just an excuse, and it may be just a last line of defense against becoming active, but still, in order to deal with it you have to address the claim. So I'm wondering . . .

There is a sense in which the claim is certainly true. There certainly is something . . . human nature, that we all have. First of all, it is something we don't know much about. Doubtless there is a rich and complex human nature, and doubtless it's largely genetically determined, like everything else. But we don't know what it is. However, there's enough evidence from history and experience to show that it is certainly at least consistent with everything you mentioned.

**Since we have had the phenomena, of course they can exist alongside human nature.**
More than that. We know that human nature, and that includes our nature, yours and mine, can easily turn people into quite efficient torturers and mass murderers and slave drivers and so on. We know that. You don't have to look very far. But what does that mean? Should we therefore not try to stop torture? If we see somebody beating a child to death, should we say, "Well, you know, that's human nature"? Which it is, in fact, an emergence of behavior based on the combination of human nature and certain pressures and circumstances. There are certainly conditions under which people will act like that. But to the extent that the statement is true, and there is such an extent, it's just not relevant. Human nature also has the capacity to lead to selflessness and cooperation and sacrifice and support and solidarity and lots of other things too.

**Is there a sense in which one way of being is more consistent with human fulfillment and development and another way of being is somehow contrary to it? Where do values come from?**

Where do values come from? That's an interesting question. Any answer that we give is based on extremely little understanding, so nothing one says is very serious. But I don't see how it can fail to be true. Just from the conditions of moral judgment it seems to me that it must be true that moral values are basically rooted in our nature. The reason I say that is pretty elementary. Undoubtedly, the way in which we look at things and judge them and assess them and so on has a significant and notable cultural factor. But that aside, we are certainly capable, and everyone does, of making moral judgments and assessments and evaluations in entirely new situations. We do it all the time. We're constantly coming up with new situations. We may not consciously evaluate them, but we certainly are at least tacitly doing it. It's the basis for our choice of action. So we're constantly making all kinds of judgments, including moral and aesthetic judgments, about new things and new situations. Either it's being done just randomly, like you pull something out of a hat, which certainly doesn't seem to be true, either introspectively or by observation, or else we're doing it on the basis of some moral system that we have in our mind somehow which gives answers, or at least partial answers, to a whole range of new situations. Nobody knows what that system is. We don't understand it at all. But it seems to be rich and complex enough that it applies to indefinitely many new situations. How did it get there?

**What characterizes a system like this?**
Maybe it's an axiomatic system. I'm sure this is false. You could imagine it's like the axioms of number theory. It's a bunch of principles from which you can deduce consequences, saying this action is preferable to that one. I'm not making that as a serious proposal, but that would be what such a system could look like. Or it could be like language.

**Could you make a serious proposal?**
A serious proposal I suspect is more like what we know about language. A lot is known: that there are basic fundamental principles that are invariant, sort of fixed in our nature. They hold for all languages. They provide the framework for language. They allow a certain limited degree of modification, and that modification comes from early experience. When the options of variation are fixed, you have a whole system functioning which allows us to do exactly what you and I are doing, namely to say new things, to understand new things, to interpret new expressions nobody has ever

heard. Qualitatively speaking, that's what the system of moral judgment looks like. So it's conceivable that it has a similar kind of basis. But we have to find the answer. You can't just guess. You could say the same about . . .

**It can't be simple. It can't be "Thou shalt not kill," obviously.**
No. Because that's not what we decide. We decide much more complex things. So what are they? We have good reason to believe that they're there because we can in fact make relatively consistent judgments, understood and appreciated by others, sometimes with disagreement, in which case you can have moral discourse. And it's under new conditions and facing new problems, and so on. Unless we're angels, it got into the organism the same way other complex things did, namely, largely by a genetically determined framework which gets marginally modified through the course of probably early experience. That's a moral system. How much variation can there be in such moral systems? Without understanding, we don't know. How much variation can there be in languages? Without understanding we don't know.

**By variation, you mean from individual to individual?**
Or from culture to culture, and so on. We can make a fair guess that it's not much variation. The reason for that is quite elementary. The system appears to be complex and determinate, and there are only two factors that can enter into determining it: One is our fixed internal nature, and the other is experience. And we know that experience is very impoverished. It doesn't give a lot of direction.

Suppose somebody asks, "Why do children undergo puberty at a certain age?" Actually, nobody knows the answer to that, but there are two factors that can enter into it. One is something in prepuberty experience that sets you to undergo puberty, some effect of the environment, say, peer pressure or something like that. The other is, you're just designed so that under certain conditions and at a certain level of maturation, hormones, this and that, you undergo puberty. Everybody assumes the second, without knowing anything. If somebody said they think that it's peer pressure that causes puberty because you see other people doing it and you want to be like them, without knowing anything you just laugh. The reason you laugh is very simple. The environment is not specific enough and rich enough to determine this highly specific change that takes place. That logic holds for just about everything in growth and development.

That's why people assume without knowledge that an embryo will become a chicken or a human depending on its nature, not depending on the nutrition that's fed in, though it needs the nutrition. The nutrition doesn't have enough information to cause those highly specific changes. And it looks as if things like moral judgment are of that character.

**As are, you would say, rules of language, perhaps even concepts?**
Yeah. For rules of language and for concepts, there's a fair amount of understanding of the matter, especially rules of language. In fact, that's the area of human intelligence where there's most understanding. But almost everything has more or less the same logic. As I said, it's not different from the logic of embryological development. In fact, it's kind of similar to that. I think a reasonable judgment at this point would be that things like moral evaluation are similar. Actually contributing to this is the fact that you can have moral discourse. Take an issue on which people are really split. Take, say, slavery. To a certain extent, the debate over slavery wasn't just an intellectual debate, obviously. It was a struggle. But insofar as it was an intellectual debate, and it was, partially, there was a certain shared moral ground to it. And in fact the slave owners' arguments are not so simple to answer. In fact, some of them are valid and have a lot of implications, and they were taken seriously by American workers in the late nineteenth century.

**You take better care of the slave if you own it than . . .**
Exactly. You take better care of your car if you own it than if you rent it, so you take better care of your worker if you own it than if you rent it. So slavery is benevolent. And the free market is morally atrocious. Workers who organized into the Knights of Labor and other working-class organizations in the late nineteenth century—you look back at the literature and you see a strain running through that says, "Look, we fought to end slavery, not to impose it."

**So somehow there are these moral principles or something that you understand that you have to appeal to even if what you're doing is rather venal.**
In fact, I think it's extremely rare for even an SS guard or a torturer or whatever to say, "I'm doing this because I like to be a son of a bitch." Everybody does bad things in their lives, and if you think back, it's rare that you have said, "I'm doing it because I feel like it."

**You reinterpret the components of it so . . .**
So it fits the moral values that you share with other people. I don't want to suggest that moral values are uniform; if you look across cultures you do find some differences. But when you look at different languages you also appear to find in fact radical differences. You know they can't be there. Because if the differences were really great, it would have been impossible to acquire any of the languages. So therefore they've got to be superficial, and the scientific question is: prove what must be true by the logic of the situation. I think the same things must be the case for moral judgment too. Going back to your original point, we can't reasonably doubt that moral values are rooted in our nature, I don't think.

**But if that's true, I've always had to think about it in such a way that for me the image of a human being is a creature with certain kinds of needs and desires and potentials and capabilities and that the fulfillment of those is social, that the fulfillment of those doesn't entail that one crush another, that one be on top of another; that one gain at another's loss and so on. If that's true, and if people have this shared set of values, then you have to explain why everything is as corrupt and hierarchical and war-laden as it is.**
First of all, why not ask another question: How come there is so much sympathy and care and love and solidarity? That's also true.

**That's the reverse. That's the way I answer it all the time.**
There's no such thing as "Why is there so much of this and so much of that?" There is what there is. What there is is doubtless conditioned by the opportunities and choices that are imposed and available in a particular social, cultural, and even physical setting.

**Someone might say, just to clarify what all this means, to truck and barter is human.**
Someone can say it, but there's no reason to believe it.

**Why isn't there any reason to believe it? The person's argument is, "Look around. Trucking and bartering everywhere."**
And you look at peasant societies and they lived for thousands of years without it. Take a look inside a family: Do people truck and barter over how much they're going to eat for dinner? Certainly a family is a normal

social structure. You can't exist without it. And you don't have trucking and bartering in it. If you look back at the history of trucking and bartering, say, look at the history of modern capitalism, here we know a lot about it. First of all, peasants had to be driven by force and violence into a labor system. They didn't want it. Then there were major conscious efforts made to create wants. There's a whole interesting literature about want creation. It happened over a long stretch in the evolution of capitalism, but you see it encapsulated briefly when slavery was terminated. It's dramatic to look at those cases.

**You see it all the time on TV.**
Creating wants, yes, but I'm talking about conscious discussion of the need to do it. In the early 1830s there was a big slave revolt in Jamaica, which was one of the things that led the British to decide to give up slavery, that is, it was not paying any more. Within a couple of years they had to go from a slave economy to a so-called free economy. But they wanted it to remain exactly the same. They understood this. You take a look at the parliamentary debates. They're very conscious that they've got to keep it the way it is. The masters become the owners. The slaves become the happy workers. We've got to somehow work it out.

**Distribution of wealth and power, keep it. Slave relation, dump it.**
Yes, they wanted everything to remain the same except not formal slavery, and the problem is, how do you do it? There's a lot of open land in Jamaica. If you let the slaves go free, they're just going to go out on the land and settle and be perfectly happy, and they're not going to work for the sugar plantations. How are we going to force them to work on the plantation? Two things were decided. This was the period when everybody was talking about how marvelous free trade is. The government's not allowed to intervene, and you can't help people in the Irish famine a decade away, and that sort of thing. But in Jamaica it was a little different. There they said, "We'll use government state force to close off the lands so people can't go to the land. And since all these workers don't really want a lot of things, they're just going to satisfy their needs, which they can easily do in this tropical climate, we have to create wants. We have to create a set of wants so that they desire things which they now don't desire. And the only way they'll be able to achieve those desires is by working as wage labor in order to get them." There was conscious

discussion and extensive efforts to do exactly what you see on TV: create wants so that people would be driven into a wage labor society which they don't want themselves. That pattern is done over and over again through the history of capitalism. In fact, what the history of capitalism shows is that throughout people had to be driven into situations which are now claimed to be their nature. If the history shows anything, it's that that's not their nature.

**But of course if you erase the history, erase the evidence, and look only at a snapshot of the present, it's a consistent hypothesis that maybe it is natural. It becomes a compelling legitimization.**
Sure. But again, by that argument, you could justify slavery. Take a snapshot of a slave society, and probably under most circumstances many slaves not only accept it but want it to stay that way. That's the only way they can survive. They look to the master to protect them. They don't want to give that up. Same about feudal societies. Same about absolutism. Probably the same about prisons, if you bother to look.

**So what is it about the society we live under that is at the core of what's wrong? What's got to go?**
In my opinion, every form of authority and domination and hierarchy, every authoritarian structure has to justify itself. It has no prior justification. It has to prove that it's justified.

**What kind of authoritarian structure?**
Anything.

**Something where one person has more power than another.**
Yeah. Like you stop your three-year-old kid when he's trying to cross the street. That's an authoritarian situation. It's got to be justified. Okay, I think in that case you can give a justification for it. The burden of proof is on the person exercising superiority, invariably. Most of the time, when you look, these structures have no justification. They have no moral justification. They have no justification in the interests of the person lower in the hierarchy, or other people, the environment, the future, the society, or anything else. They're there in order to preserve certain structures of power and domination that benefit those at the top. And every time you find that, it's illegitimate and it should change. And we find it everywhere.

We find it in all kinds of human relations, crucially in economic relations, which are at the core of how any society functions. What's produced, what's consumed, what's distributed, what decision was made. These things help set a framework within which everything else happens. And they're completely hierarchic and authoritarian.

**It's also true that how people live their lives in their homes, how people regard one another sets a framework in which even work is affected. All these things mutually interact with each other and affect one another.** And in every one of them that you look at are questions about authority and domination that ought to be raised constantly, and that very rarely have satisfactory answers. Sometimes they do, I think, but it has to be shown. As a matter of fact, you can even ask the same about your relation to animals. The questions can be asked there too, and in fact are being asked.

**You're an animal rights activist?**
I think it's a serious question: To what extent do we have a right to torture animals? I think it's a very good thing that that question . . .

**Torture?**
Experiments are torturing animals, let's say. That's what they are. So to what extent do we have a right to torture animals for our own good? I think that's not a trivial question.

**What about eating?**
Same question.

**Are you a vegetarian?**
I'm not, but I think it's a serious question. If you want my guess, my guess would be that . . .

**A hundred years from now everyone will be.**
I don't know if it's a hundred years, but it seems to me if history continues—it's not at all obvious that it will—but if society continues to develop without catastrophe on something like the course that you can sort of see over time, I wouldn't be in the least surprised if it moves toward vegetarianism and protection of animal rights. In fact, what we've seen over

the years—and it's hard to be optimistic in the twentieth century, which is one of the worst centuries in human history in terms of atrocities and terror and so on—but still, over the years, including the twentieth century, there is a widening of the moral realm, bringing in broader and broader domains of individuals who are regarded as moral agents.

**Nothing could be happening to that underlying, wired-in, innate, intrinsic character . . . that can't be changing.**
No, but it can get more and more realized. You can get a better and better understanding of it. We're self-conscious beings. We're not rocks. And we can get more and more understanding of our own nature, not because we read a book about it. The book doesn't have anything to tell you, because nobody knows anything. But just through experience, including historical experience, which is part of our own personal experience because it's embedded in our culture, which we enter into.

**So then it's plausible that vegetarians, animal rights advocates, and the like are just a couple of steps ahead in discerning something about . . .**
It's possible. I think I'd certainly keep an open mind on that. You can understand how it could be true. It's certainly a pretty intelligible idea to us. I think one can see the moral force to it. You don't have to go back very far to find gratuitous torture of animals. In Cartesian philosophy, for example, where it was assumed . . . the Cartesians thought they had proven that humans had minds and everything else in the world was a machine. So there's no difference between a cat and a watch, let's say, it's just the cat's a little more complicated. You go back to the court in the seventeenth century, and big smart guys who studied all that stuff and thought they understood it would, as a sport, take Lady So-and-So's favorite dog and kick it and beat it to death and laugh, saying, "This silly lady doesn't understand the latest philosophy," which was that it was just like dropping a rock on the floor. That's gratuitous torture of animals. It was regarded as if we would ask a question about the torturing of a rock. You can't do it. There's no way to torture a rock. The moral sphere has certainly changed in that respect. Gratuitous torture of animals is no longer considered quite legitimate.

**Maybe what's changing is the understanding of what an animal is, rather than some of the underlying moral values.**

In that case it probably was, because in fact the Cartesian view was a departure from the traditional view, in which you didn't torture animals gratuitously. On the other hand, there are cultures like, say, fox hunting, aristocratic cultures that have fox hunting as a sport or, say, bear baiting or things like that, in which there actually was gratuitous torture of animals. In fact, it's kind of intriguing to see how we regard this. Take cockfighting, in which cocks are trained to tear each other to shreds. Our culture happens to regard that as barbaric. On the other hand, we train humans to tear each other to shreds—it's called boxing. And that's not regarded as barbaric. So there are things we don't permit of cocks that we permit of poor people. There are some funny values at work there.

**It's peculiar. But of course we don't pay the birds, whereas we pay the boxers. We assume that they suffer.**
But everybody knows that you don't find people going into professional boxing from wealthy families. That tells you something right away.

**So if authority relations are the things that are suspect, the things that have to be undone, what are the institutions that basically embody that? Presumably private ownership.**
Private ownership's an obvious one. Patriarchic relations are another. Relations of race discrimination and oppression are others.

**How about the market?**
The market itself, just by its very logic, induces oppressive relations very quickly, simply because of the inequities it produces.

**That's where the justice or equity in some sense is the thing that's abrogated by authority, the thing that you want to justify.**
I think authority and justice are incompatible, except in very rare instances, namely, if the authority can be justified. And maybe sometimes it can. Like the case of caring for children. I think there it can be justified. Or suppose we had a catastrophe, let's say. Suppose a hurricane swept over this place and a couple of people who for some reason happened to have their heads screwed on, sort of took control and told us, "Do this, do that, do the other thing." I'd follow them. I wouldn't know what to do. If they seemed to understand what has to be done, had presence of mind, some understanding of the situation, I think I would willingly grant them the

authority to make decisions that I don't feel competent to make, and I'd rather have them make them. So I grant them the authority to do it. That's a situation of authority. But we agree to it.

**Suppose somebody comes along and says that most working people in fact are granting the authority of their employers and bosses on the grounds that they don't have the expertise, the knowledge, and skills, and they also don't want the burden and the responsibility?**
I would ask the same question that we would ask of prisoners. Suppose somebody said the prisoners are voluntarily granting the authority to the guards. I'd believe that when it's proven. The burden of proof, again, is always on the person who claims that the authority is justified. I think that's a fundamental moral principle.

**Sure, but if you want to make a counterargument . . .**
It's not that simple. Let's make it realistic. The way things are now, and this has been true throughout modern history, people have chosen to go to jail because they can survive. If you're starving to death on the outside, freezing to death, there are cases right now where they go out and break a window and say, "Hey, put me in jail." It looks like he's choosing to be kicked around by the warden.

**Because it's better than another horrible situation.**
It's true in a sense.

**It's also true that people choose to work for employers who will exploit them because there's no other option.**
You have to look at the range of options that are not only objectively available to them, but that are subjectively available. How are they allowed to think? How are they able to think? There are all kinds of ways of thinking that are kind of cut off from us, not because we're incapable of them, but there are various blockages that have been developed and imposed that keep us from thinking about them. Actually, that's what indoctrination is about. And I don't mean somebody giving you lectures. Sitcoms on television, sports that you watch—every aspect of the culture involves some form of expression of what a proper life or a proper set of values are, implicitly. That's all indoctrination, and that cuts off opportunities. If people cannot find what their own values are except through interaction,

what's called political theory, there's not much theory to it, it's truisms, but one of the traditional ideas of political theory for hundreds of years has been that in order to maintain absolute control—what we nowadays call totalitarian societies—what you have to do is isolate people. People have to be isolated in order to be controlled. And once they're isolated they're easily controlled because they don't even know what they think. You're sitting alone in a room and you don't even know what you think. Again, in science it's a commonplace. You work together. There's no other way to work. In order to have ideas or understanding, you have to sort of bounce them off other people and see what their reactions are and learn from them. That's the way you even find out what your values are, or your interests, or anything else. Keep people isolated and they don't have subjective options, even if they have objective ones. And unless those options are opened up, both subjectively and in fact concretely, namely you can do something about it without suicide or suffering, then to claim that people choose their oppression is completely meaningless. They choose it under conditions where there isn't a choice.

**Suppose somebody said that that kind of observation is taken from on high. Who are you to decide that what somebody else is choosing has been constrained? Who are you to decide? Once you start doing that . . .** It's for them to decide, I agree. I think it's for the people to decide. But the point is the people should be given every opportunity to make a considered choice, meaning an opportunity to think through the options and so on. For example, I've just been reading a novel by an Egyptian novelist who won the Nobel Prize a couple of years ago [Naguib Mahfouz], about life in Cairo, I think it was in the 1920s. The central story is a woman who lives under the iron rule of her husband. She's a total slave. In a big tragedy, she gets kicked out for this or that infringement. Her life is destroyed because she loved being a slave. She was able to take care of the house, and she had her domain in which she was not out of the house, but that's okay, because the husband is the god. You can imagine the rest. Did she choose that? I'm sure it's an accurate depiction of some societies. Did she choose it? In a sense, yes. Is it therefore her nature? In order to know the answer to that question, you have to put that same person in other circumstances.

**People have a remarkable talent for making the best of whatever situation they're in, and that's obviously a tremendous advantage. But it's also**

a quality that leaves you trapped in circumstances far less desirable than you might otherwise attain.

That's the point of isolation—cut people off from thinking through and perceiving the opportunities that are available to them. Leave them only making do with things as they are.

**So suppose we eliminate these obstacles to human beings being free and liberated and fulfilling themselves. What does that mean? What kind of a society is that? Clearly, there's been one label given to this—socialism— over the years. But nowadays people claim this failed, that something went wrong.**

First of all, I don't know that anything went wrong. We may not be ready for it, but there was a period in history when we weren't ready for ending slavery, either. There was a period in human history when conditions, including subjective conditions, were such that ending slavery wasn't in the cards. You could argue—I don't agree with it—one could argue that conditions are such that we need the degree of hierarchy and domination that exists in totalitarian institutions like capitalist enterprises in order to satisfy our needs, at least so far in history.

**With central planning or dictatorship . . .**

It could be argued. I don't believe a word of it. But the point is somebody would have to argue it. If you look at what actually happened, the concentration of force and violence was such as to guarantee certain outcomes. Those outcomes destroyed incipient efforts at cooperative worker control, say. There have been efforts in that direction for hundreds of years. They regularly get crushed. And they get crushed by force. The Bolsheviks are a perfectly good example. In the stages leading up to the Bolshevik revolution, up to October 1917, there were incipient socialist institutions being developed: workers' councils, things like that. They survived to an extent, but not very long. They were pretty much eliminated. You can argue about the justification, but the fact is that they were pretty quickly eliminated. Some people want to justify it. The standard justification is that Lenin and Trotsky had to do it because of the contingencies of the civil war and survival and this and that.

**"There wouldn't have been food otherwise," says the apologist.**

Right. That's the only kind of justification that immoral acts can possibly get. That's the only kind of justification that authority can ever get. "Look, we needed it." It's like my hurricane example. Under dire conditions you accept authority.

**Actually, it's exactly analogous to the hurricane example.**
Exactly analogous. The question is, "Is it true?" There you've got to look at the historical facts. I don't think it's true. In fact, I think these structures were dismantled before the . . .

**Yes, they were, but does a Lenin or a Trotsky sincerely feel that they're like the couple of people who are running through the streets helping in the hurricane, or are they just aggrandizing their own wealth and power and status? Or it is the same thing?**
I think it's the same thing. We don't want to be cavalier about it. It's a question of historical fact and what the people really were like and what they were thinking, and you've got to find out what the answer is. But my feeling is, reading their own writings, that they knew what they were doing and it was understandable, and they even had a theory behind it. It was both a moral theory and a socioeconomic theory. First of all, as good orthodox Marxists, they didn't really believe that a socialist revolution was possible in Russia, which was just a peasant backwater. So they were carrying out a kind of holding action, waiting for the iron laws of history to grind out the revolution in Germany, where it's supposed to come. You know the story better than I do. That's what's supposed to happen by historical necessity, so they're going to hold on until it happens, and then Russia will be more backward than it ought to be. Well, it didn't happen in Germany.

They also thought that in this precapitalist society, Russia being a deeply impoverished Third World society, basically precapitalist, except for little pockets here and there, it was just necessary to beat the people into development. They had to be turned into what Trotsky called the "labor army" in order to carry out forced development, which would somehow carry them over the early stages of capitalism and industrialization to the point where then the iron laws of history would start to work because the master said they were going to. So there was a theory behind it and a moral principle: It's going to be better for them in a while.

So these could be understandable and even honest mistakes, or they could be natural outgrowths of a worldview which says there are relatively few people who are exceptionally smart and should run the show.

That was Bakunin's prediction, about half a century before, that this was exactly what was going to happen. He was talking about the Marxists at that time. That was before Lenin was born. His prediction was that the nature of the intelligentsia as a formation in modem industrial society was that they could become managers. They're not going to become managers because they own capital or a lot of guns. They're going to become managers because they can control and organize and direct what's called knowledge and so on.

**Information and skills and access to decision-making.**
And he says they're going to become a Red bureaucracy, because that's in their interests. He didn't say that's the nature of people. I don't know how much he thought it through. But reading back, we shouldn't say they are going to do it because that's the nature of people. It's that the ones who don't do it will be cast by the wayside. The ones who do it will make out. The ones who are worthless and brutal and harsh enough to do it are going to survive in this kind of system. The ones who try to associate themselves with popular organizations and to help the people themselves become organized and to serve the people and that kind of thing are just not going to survive in these situations of power.

**Supposing you have a relative advantage on information and knowledge: How do you explain that to yourself? It's not too dissimilar from having a great amount of wealth, material wealth: You either have that material wealth or knowledge by virtue of somehow being better or by somehow unjustly having more than you deserve. It's a lot easier to assume that it because you're better.**
Why is it "better"?

**You're in the lead.**
But all kinds of people are better at all kinds of things. There are things that I think I'm better at than the guy across the street. There are things that the guy across the street's better at than I am. Who's better?

**You have a healthy view of the situation. There's an unhealthy view of the situation that says, "The reason I have three cars and a huge house is that I am a different kind of human being. I am superior." It's like racism, except it doesn't have skin color as its . . .**

Everyone has some particular distribution of traits. You're better at some things and worse at others. This guy is a good violinist. This guy can't hear straight. This guy can fix mechanical things and understand them. The other one can't. If it wasn't true, I'd want to commit suicide. Living in a society of clones would be worse than death. If everybody was alike, it's not like living at all. You should enjoy and appreciate the variety. The fact that other people can do things that I can't do is a source of appreciation. I don't feel bad if I can't play the violin like somebody else. If I can't solve physics problems like somebody else, fine. It makes me happy. You do what you do. The particular distribution of traits that I have, partly just by nature, partly by the advantages that I've had through life, which were plenty, in the case of the guy with three cars, there's a particular collection of traits plus luck. The traits might be viciousness, aggressiveness, willingness to undercut others, and so on. Whatever that collection of traits is, they're the ones that are valued and supported in particular social arrangements. So the Mafia don has traits which are rewarded under particular social situations. Hitler had traits which were rewarded under those social situations. That part's true, in that sense. It doesn't mean that they're better. It means that they're better adapted to getting ahead under particular conditions.

**The person in that position can have your understanding of the situation or can have an understanding of the situation that it's just basically theft or can understand the situation as a proper reward for somebody who is a superior being.**

Usually people will pick the last one.

**Right. That's my point. But once you pick the last one if you're Lenin or Trotsky or whoever, then the understanding of society that you come up with tends to reflect that. So you come up with yourself as a central actor, even a savior. You think, "There's a hurricane coming, and I have to save everybody from it," when in fact there is no hurricane coming, or, in any event, the only solution is for people to be saving themselves, not**

having you take away their means to do so. There was the possibility of
real democracy and real participation instead. But you see a hurricane
because the role of savior is the one you want to fill.

And that's where I come back to what I said before. The burden of proof
is always on the person who claims the right of authority. So if you see a
hurricane coming, prove it. If you can convince me that there's a hurricane coming, and that you're the person who ought to direct people, okay,
maybe so. But you've got to prove it. I don't have to disprove it. I don't have
to disprove anything. I can just say, "You haven't proven it. Period." And
then I win.

**And beating you over the head till you agree or holding all the cards and
allowing no one to play unless they agree is of course not proving it, it
is coercing it . . .**

Yes, and so that's the sense in which the burden of proof is on those who
claim the legitimacy of authority. And that's true whether it's a factory, a
family, or any other social arrangement. I think that that burden can rarely
be met. It seems to me that part of real education, if we ever allowed such a
thing, would be to make sure people understand early on that that's where
the burden of proof is. I think you don't have to try to teach it to people,
however. I think they know it. You have to keep it from being driven out
of their heads. And it is driven out of their heads. It's driven out of their
heads early on just by the structure of the educational system. Kids who
are too independent quickly get into trouble and are kept in line. Again,
we don't want to be glib about it. Again, the burden of proof is always on
whoever it is that claims that the child has to be controlled. Maybe the
child is being independent and should be encouraged. It's just personal
experience.

As a kid I happened to be lucky enough to be, until I was about twelve,
in an experimental school run on Deweyite lines by Temple University,
which happened to be a very free and open and independent place where
they encouraged independence and creativity and so on. It was very constructive. It was a shock to me when I got into City Academic High School
for upward-striving kids who were going to go off to big colleges and discovered what authority really is like in educational structures. I never had
that before. And it certainly requires justification, and I doubt that justification can be given in a great many cases. A lot of even the stupidity of

education has a social function, namely, preventing independence. You're given some stupid assignment in eighth grade, and you'd better obey.

**I've noticed that the public school system teaches not just obedience but also endurance of boredom, the ability to sit and watch the clock and not run out of the room, which of course is exactly the skill that one has to have to work in a capitalist firm.**

Punctuality. My oldest friend, who happened to emigrate from Eastern Europe when he was fifteen or so, once told me that he went to a school in New York for bright kids. One of the things that struck him right off in comparison with his earlier education was that if you got a C on an exam, nobody paid any attention. But if you came two minutes late, you had to go to the principal's office—meaning you're being trained for docility, obedience, punctuality, for an assembly-line job.

**I remember even at MIT I was always astounded by the extent to which the education was faculty coming in, writing textbooks on the wall, and never once talking about the creative aspect of what they do or doing it with you, but rather just reproducing stuff that you could go off and read in any event.**

It surprises me when you say that.

**As an undergraduate.**

In graduate school it's just not like that at all. In fact, graduate school is kind of like an apprenticeship. You're working together.

**Clearly that's the mode of education that makes some sense. The words are horrible: "master" and "apprentice," but the reality is interesting.**

It's because you're learning a craft. Apprenticeship doesn't mean necessarily following orders. You can contribute and have your own ideas and learn at the same time. Doing science properly just isn't something you can teach. No one knows how to teach it. You just kind of get the idea somehow. It's like learning how to ride a bike or build a table. The way you get the idea is by working with people who somehow got the idea. You get something from them, and in science certainly you contribute to them. Everybody knows in the sciences that an awful lot of good ideas are coming from young people. That's just standard.

**All your ideas come from students.**
It's just not even a question. You just take it for granted.

**So you get the ideas from the students. Supposing we had a society with no authority, where's the drive? Where's the momentum? Where's the pressure to advance and grow? These are questions this discussion probably raises for some people.**
First of all, the "pressure to advance"—you have to ask what that means. If you mean the pressure to produce more, who wants it? Is that necessarily the right thing to do? That's not obvious. In many areas it's probably the wrong thing to do.

**Therefore, the criticism that having this degree of freedom will remove that type of pressure isn't criticism at all; it's a compliment.**
Let's go back to the period when people had to be driven. It's still today. People have to be driven to have certain wants. Why? Why not leave them alone so they can just be happy and do other things? The only drive there ought to be internal. Take a look at kids: They're creative. They explore. They want to find out everything, try out new things. Why does a kid walk?

**They have plenty of energy, curiosity, desire, but they don't want to work themselves to death.**
Why does a kid walk? Say you've got a kid who's a year old. He's crawling fine. He can get across the room really fast, so fast his parents run after him to keep him from knocking everything down. All of a sudden he gets up and starts walking. He's terrible at walking. He walks one step and falls on his face. If he wants to really get somewhere, he's going to crawl. So why does the kid start walking? To do new things. That's the way we're built. We're built to want to do new things, even if they're not efficient, even if they're harmful, even if you get hurt. I don't think that ever stops. You want to explore and press your capacities to the limits. You want to appreciate what you can do. The joy of creation is something very few people have circumstances to experience much. Artists have it. Craftspeople have it. Scientists have it. Most people don't have the opportunity often, in our society. But if you've been lucky enough to have that opportunity, you know it's quite an experience. It doesn't have to be discovering Einstein's theory of relativity.

Your way of expressing it is so different from ... I remember—we won't use names—a physicist at MIT who gave a big talk and described the pleasure and the joy of creativity and wished that so many people, 99 percent of the population, who don't have the capacity to experience that and to enjoy that, could have that capacity. But since they don't, I'll at least try to convey to them the pleasure that I get out of having a new idea.

I think that the physicist didn't want to think. Whoever it was knows perfectly well that anyone can have that pleasure and that whoever it was had that pleasure many times in his life just by seeing what other people have done.

You can also have it at many different levels of ...

When you read a proof and finally figure out what it's about, it's exciting.

And it could be the Pythagorean theorem ... tenth grade as well as quantum mechanics or whatever ...

That's exciting. My God, I never understood that before! That's creativity, even if somebody proved it two thousand years ago. Every physicist has gone through that plenty of times. You keep being struck by the marvels of what you're discovering, and you're discovering it, even though somebody else did it already. And if you can add little bits to that here and there, that's exciting. I don't have any reason to believe what that physicist said ... And I think the same is true of a person who builds a boat. I don't see what's fundamentally any different.

It doesn't seem to be any different at all as far as creativity and pleasure of accomplishment, etc., unless of course an onus is put on it.

I wish I could do that. I can't. I can't imagine doing it.

But there's one sense in which it's different. That is there's a social difference between those kinds of acts that can accrue power and the kinds that won't. The skills of building a boat are different than the skills of say, conducting a meeting. Or for that matter being compelling verbally is very different than, say, running quickly, at least in most societies.

But the skills to which rewards and power accrue are violence ...

I don't mean necessarily in a bad society. Even in a good society the person who can make an argument and express herself well is going to be more influential if that isn't equalized somehow. It's relatively equalized. The person who runs fast but has no verbal abilities whatsoever, how's the person . . . ?

I don't think it's true. I've been in situations, and I'm sure you have, when I knew I was presenting the right argument, but I couldn't convince anybody. Because they decided to do something else. It happens all the time. It happens in personal life, family arguments, social situations, and so on. Unless the person who—maybe some Martian watching this can say, "Jones won the argument." But unless Jones has the power to implement it, it doesn't make any difference.

If you're working with a group, some kind of organization, a business, or whatever it might happen to be, suppose there is a degree of equity and fairness, at least formal, with regard to decision-making, and you all sit around and make decisions. One or two people have knowledge of how the whole operation works and have at their fingertips a whole lot of information and facts about what's going on and also are very verbal, and some of the other people have productive skills and various other skills that are associated with the business but don't have that information at their disposal. There isn't any doubt in my mind who's going to win nine times out of ten.

Win what?

Policy decisions.

The policy decisions. And who will win the decisions about how it's actually implemented? The people with the productive skills.

No. Not necessarily at all.

Why not? They're the ones who are going to do it in a society with equity. We were assuming a society with equity. Nobody has any power. They just have different capacities.

One person, one vote.

All right, the person who makes the more convincing argument, assuming rationality, should convince the others. But then the person who implements the decisions will do it their own way.

**Clearly the situation will be much better if everybody comes to a decision with a degree of confidence and skills and so on that's commensurate to participating.**
That's what it means by being convinced. If you are convinced that this is the right thing to do, it doesn't make any difference whether somebody else had the idea or you had the idea. You're equally convinced. If you're not convinced, something went wrong. Then it was a situation of power and not a matter of greater capacity to work things out.

**Take a Yugoslav firm in the market system. The workers appoint a manager who makes a whole array of decisions that are the same as a manager would make in the Ford Motor Company. The workers in fact agree that the manager's decisions make sense and should be implemented. They can't make the decisions themselves, necessarily, because they don't have access to the facts. Still the situation is pretty disgusting.**
There's a situation where there's a difference of power, and the power translates into access to . . .

**What if the formal power rests with the workers?**
There's already a presupposition: The manager had more information and the manager got that because the manager had more power. Otherwise the manager wouldn't have had more information.

**The manager's job is to oversee all this information and put the stuff together. But if you divide jobs up that way, you're imposing relations of power. Exactly. That's what I'm getting at.**
But if we extract the power from the situation it won't be true. If everyone has the same access to information, it still may turn out that the guy who happens to be the manager comes up with the best idea and everybody says, "Yeah, that's the best idea." Okay, fine. That's not a problem. We know that it's not going to happen consistently. There's one area of human life that I know of which kind of approximates an equitable situation. It isn't really equitable, but it approximates one. That's a scientific laboratory, a scientific enterprise, where you have a senior professor who won a Nobel Prize and you have an undergraduate assistant, a lab technician, and so on. If it's really working well, there's a lot of cooperation. And you see it. It is not the case that the person with the more publications comes up with all

the answers, by no means. If they're really working together and trying to achieve something . . .

**Then it's a collective, or something. If you don't have structurally imposed differences in decision-making power or in access to information needed for developing agendas and positions, fine.**
It may be that the guy with the Nobel Prize will often come up with a good idea. Maybe not. In fact, in these situations it typically isn't the case. It's often the graduate student.

**After they've got a Nobel Prize, they're already too old.**
Probably. Or they're too stuck in their ways. But the senior professor often has a contribution to make that's unique: experience, remembering something that somebody did four years ago that nobody else ever heard of. There are all kinds of ways in which people contribute to collective decisions. I don't see any reason to believe that, say, a decision in a factory is so infinitely more complex than working on an advanced scientific problem that you can expect one person to always have the right ideas. That's not going to happen. If it happens, it's because of power differences.

**An imbalance in access to decision making or information or skills critical to it . . .**
And then we're back to where we were: eliminate the power differences or strive to eliminate them.

**Let me switch gears a minute, back to the question of animal rights, the broadening understanding of human values, and all that. How do you react to the debate around abortion?**
I think it's a hard one. I don't think the answers are simple. It's a case where there really are conflicting values. Most human situations, the kinds of things we're in all the time, it's rare that there's a clear and simple answer. Sometimes the answers are very murky because we have different values and they just conflict. At least our understanding of our own moral values is not like an axiomatic system, where there's an answer and not some other answer. There are what appear to be conflicting values which give different answers. Maybe because we don't understand them well enough, or maybe they really are in conflict. In this case they're straight conflicts. From one point of view, a child up to a point is an organ of the mother's

body. The mother ought to have the decision what to do. And that's true. From another point of view, the organism is a potential human being, and it has rights. And those two things are in conflict.

One biologist I know once pointed out that you could say the same thing about women washing their hands. If a woman washes her hands, lots of cells flake off, and in principle those cells have the genetic instructions for a human being. You can imagine a future technology which would take one of them and create a human being from it. He was making it as a reductio ad absurdum argument, but because there's an element of truth to it, an element so tiny that it makes it a reductio ad absurdum argument, but it's not like saying something about astrology. What he's saying is true.

**There's a related argument I've found tough to deal with. Suppose you have a person who is a surgeon who is so skilled she is the only one who can deal with this particular kind of ailment. There's a sudden outbreak of the ailment. It only takes five minutes for the person to do what they do, but only they can do it. So you could literally have an assembly line because there are so many people struck with this ailment, an assembly line of people flowing past this person. So if this person goes to the bathroom or goes to eat a meal or goes to do anything, more people are going to die that would have been saved had she not done that. What this person supposed to do?**

It's like triage. A person is going to have to make an impossible choice among alternatives. It's easy to construct situations like that. That's what they do in philosophy seminars all the time. We don't agree with torture. There was an article in *Newsweek* by a philosopher whose hidden agenda was that you shouldn't criticize Israel for torturing Arabs. The argument was like an elementary philosophy seminar. People say torture is bad, but is it really bad? Suppose there was a doomsday machine that was about to go off and blow up the universe. There was one person who knew how to stop it, but he wasn't telling us how to stop it. The only way you would get it out of him was by torturing him. Under those circumstances, would torture be okay? You say, "Okay, under those circumstances." Then, aha! You're not opposed to torture. Let's move it a little bit over. You get into what's called a slippery-slope argument. You can play this game all the time. You can make up situations in which usually conflicting values lead to what would ordinarily be ridiculous conclusions under other circumstances. And the trouble is, life often poses such circumstances. You don't have to make them up. The abortion issue is one where life is posing those choices.

**You think that the choice there isn't that it is or isn't a person. You just basically have to admit that it's a potential person, it's an actual organ in a sense.**
We don't have a clear conception of what a person is. I think a reasonable proposal is that it changes from an organ to a person when it's viable. But that's arguable and it's not clear when it is. That's why this biologist pointed out it could be when the woman was washing her hands, depending on the state of technology. But that's life. You're faced with hard decisions of conflicting values.

**Changing gears again: Take the last thirty years, say, from the New Left to the present, and look at it as a span of political activism in the US. Leftists seem to do this, as far as I can tell, very infrequently. Try and basically say, "What lessons are there in that? Is whatever we achieved the most we could have achieved? Did the people who were acting, were they doing basically about as well as one could expect, or were there horrible failures? Was there some impediment that was being overlooked, some obstacle to having greater success that we just didn't think of and we didn't deal with, and had we dealt with that we would have done better?" In other words, how do you view the period? Certainly people of my generation, a great many of them, right now are very frustrated. They're feeling like, "Thirty years ago I made this choice. It's thirty years later and it hasn't gone where I thought it was going to go."**
I think, first of all, where they thought it was going to go was pretty unrealistic. I think if you look at what's happened in thirty years, it's a lot better than it was. A lot of this stuff got started during the Vietnam War. At the ideological level, all of us who were opposed to the war lost flat out within the mainstream institutions. The question now is: have the Vietnamese done enough to compensate us for the crimes that they committed against us? In the newspapers or the journals or the books that's the only question you're allowed to discuss. If you want to be part of the educated culture, the elite culture, the only question you can pose. I actually have been through a lot of the newspapers on this, out of curiosity. Also the POW issue. George [H.W.] Bush could get up and say, "The Vietnamese should

understand that we bear them no permanent grudge. We're not going to make them pay for everything they did to us. If they finally come clean and devote their entire lives and every last resource they have to searching for the remains of one of those people they viciously blew out of the sky, then maybe we'll allow them entry into the civilized world." And there won't be one editorial writer or columnist who will either fall on the floor laughing or else say, "This guy's worse than the Nazis." Because that's the way they all are. The only issue is: Will we forgive them for the crimes they committed against us? So at that level, we just lost the whole discussion. On the other hand, let's go to the general population. To this day, after twenty-five years of this endless, unremitting propaganda, to which no response is ever tolerated, 70 percent of the population disagrees with the elite culture. That tells you there's a victory at this level. If 70 percent of the population, after all this brainwashing, still says, as late as 1990, the war was fundamentally wrong and immoral, not a mistake, then something got through.

**Absolutely. And it tells us that for a period of six, seven years, however many years, the activism that people engaged in had a tremendous and long-lasting effect. But it doesn't answer people's concern that after thirty years the size of our organizations, the degree of organized dissent, the ability to amass new movements when new crises arise, or even, much more important, the ability to have sustained movements which are striking at ongoing institutional structures, on these axes there doesn't seem to be . . .**

I think that's an inaccurate reading of history. In fact, I think the opposite is the case. The last big such crisis was the Gulf War. I just disagree with a lot of my friends on that one, including most activists on the left. They regarded what happened as a catastrophe for the Left, and as a proof of what you just said. I regard it as the opposite. This is the first time in history that I know of that big demonstrations started before a war. Take a look at the Vietnam War. After all, Kennedy started bombing South Vietnam in 1961–62. It was years before there was significant opposition.

**That was my impression too. I was incredulous at the speed at which the movement was able to make itself felt, visibly, around the Gulf . . .**

It was unbelievable. The thing that we should remember is, people in power know it. They might not want us to know it, but they know it. It's even clear from their own documents, as well as from what they do. The day the ground combat started in the Gulf War a very important document leaked. It was sort of buried in the papers, and most people missed it. It was the last paragraph of an article on something else. They leaked an early Bush administration planning document on Third World intervention. What it said was—and it still holds—that in the case of confrontations with much weaker enemies—meaning anyone we're willing to fight—we must not only defeat them but we must defeat them decisively and rapidly because anything else will undercut political support. That's a tremendous victory for the Left. These guys understand that they don't have the option to carry out intervention unless they carry out decisive, rapid victories over totally defenseless enemies before anyone notices, after having first demonized them.

**I agree with you completely about the speed and scale of the response. Yet it is the case that you describe having to argue with most of your friends. I encountered the same situation. It's a remarkable fact that we don't seem to be able to perceive, as a movement or as a body of people, our own effectively.**
Of course nobody wants you to see it. In order to perceive it, it's as if you lived in a world where everybody told you television, radio, books, everything else—that the world is flat. It's Winston Smith in 1984. He's trying to hold on to the truth that two plus two equals four. Everybody says two plus two equals five. He remembers that two plus two equals four. It's hard to hold on to that truth, especially when you're isolated.

**So what's the trick?**
The trick is not to be isolated. If you're isolated, like Winston Smith, you're sooner or later going to break, as he finally broke. That was the point of Orwell's story. That's the whole tradition of totalitarianism: Keep people isolated and you can get them to believe anything. The genius of American democracy has been to tolerate the formal freedoms that have been won through popular struggle but to eliminate any substance from them by just isolating people. And people are isolated. They're stuck in front of the tube. There are no associations. That's part of the fervor behind getting rid of unions: They're one of the natural means—not the only one—by which ordinary people come together. So you've got to destroy them. That's one of the reasons why it's very important that we

CHOMSKY RAPS WITH MICHAEL ALBERT

have no real political parties, because people could get together and do stuff.

**But what it says is that a Left which creates a culture and creates the possibility of actually working together, being friends, communicating with one another, will be much less susceptible to this coercion. When I consider now versus thirty years ago, I have this feeling that's there a fundamental change, as atomized as it was then, it is much more so now. People just don't have friends. Nobody has people who they trust, who they're friends with, who they interact with on a regular, ongoing basis. Not nobody, but there's much less of that there was then.**

I'm not so sure there's less of it. I suspect that there's probably more of it, but it's in different circles. So, for example, take the big movements of the last ...

**I'm not talking about movements. I'm talking about just normal, everyday life. My parents, my friends, all the people I know.**

So what about the people in Witness for Peace, for example? They're mostly church-based, and their friends and associations are usually through churches, often even fundamentalist churches. But they have real friends and associations and work together.

**That's one of those institutions ...**

But these things bring in huge numbers of people. That's why I say I think it's shifted. In fact, it's shifted towards different sectors of the population. In fact, they've become a lot more mainstream. During the 1960s, it was kind of kids at universities who were the ones who had these associations and the political activism to a significant extent. There was a lot of that. Not everything, of course, but that was quite a bit of it. It's true, there are things that have in fact declined. But other parts of society have increased and are deepened.

**The Left has never offered it per se. The Communist Party did once upon a time. But the modern Left, from the New Left to now has offered rallies and demonstrations. It's offered teach-ins and talks, but it's never offered ...**

What do you call the ... what do you think the right name is for these church-based Central America solidarity groups? Are they "left?" I would call it left.

**They are setting a better model, perhaps, than anything that the Left has had to offer**

I don't think they're all that separate. A lot of people in them are people who came through 1960s experiences, which affected everything. They affected the whole culture very broadly. The reason that so many things grow out of the churches is that that's the one kind of organic institution that hasn't been destroyed. They don't come out of labor unions in the country because we don't have unions. If I give a talk in Europe, up till pretty recently, even now, it could often be in a union hall. Not necessarily labor people, but just community people. I can't remember ever having done that in the US. It's usually a church. That exists. That's the one institution that hasn't been destroyed. So the movement offices are in the basement of some church. They're around.

**That's always been true.**

Because that's the only thing that's around. But out of that have come other things, people who would not regard themselves . . . they never read a Marxist-Leninist book in their lives and they don't care. Maybe their background is liberation theology. I think that's part of our movement, at least I've always regarded it that way. And the same with people who are involved in all sorts of other issues.

**To what extent would you consider yourself somehow part of the same movement as Marxist-Leninists?**

There are personal friendships and contacts, but I don't really feel much empathy with it. For one thing I don't understand a lot of it. What I do understand I usually don't like. I don't want to say that I haven't learned anything from them or that I don't hold personal relations; in fact I do support all of the groups and will continue to as long as they do things I like. But I do feel a certain closeness . . . the beliefs of the church-based groups are just incomprehensible to me, but I do feel a certain empathy with them that I don't feel with what are called official left groups.

**You'd rather have them at your side, in some sense.**

Yeah. Like when I went down to Nicaragua and I lived in the Jesuit house. I was wondering, what the heck am I doing here? But that's where I felt at home.

**They were ethical.**
Some sort of shared values. For me personally it was sort of weird, because just out of personal experience, aside from having nothing to do with organized religion or anything, I happened to grow up in an area in Philadelphia which was Irish and German Catholic, mostly. We were the only Jewish family around. I grew up with a visceral fear of Catholics. They're the people who beat you up on your way to school. So I knew when they came out of that building down the street, which was the Jesuit school, they were raving anti-Semites. So childhood memories took a long time to overcome.

**As long as we're switching over, we have the church as an institution being a possible place where people can talk, develop ideas, develop agendas. But what about the church as an impediment to social change?**
That's what it's been through most of its history. What was remarkable in the thirty, forty, fifty years is a radical change in the Catholic Church, which also showed up in many of the Protestant churches. There was a big change. The reason why the US launched this terrorist war in Central America was to destroy this. People now talk as if the big enemy is Islamic fundamentalism, but they're forgetting something: For the last ten years the big enemy has been the Catholic Church, more of an enemy than Islamic fundamentalism. They had to destroy it. When Americas Watch did their wrap-up study on the 1980s, they pointed out that it was a decade framed by the murder of the archbishop in 1980 and the murder of six Jesuit intellectuals in 1989. That wasn't accidental. The main target of attack was the church, because it had become a part, not entirely, but part of it had become a church devoted to liberation, to the poor. Sectors of the church did undertake what they called the preferential option for the poor, and very consciously. They recognized that for hundreds of years it had been the church of the rich and the oppressors, who were telling the poor, "This is your fate. Accept it." A critically important sector of the church changed, important enough to include the dominant elements among the Latin American bishops, which set off the atrocities over the last ten years, in which the US has vigorously participated.

**The change is just an accident of history?**
I don't know enough about the internal dynamics of it to explain it.

**What do you think religion is?**

Obviously, it means something to people, a lot. It doesn't to me. I don't understand it. I sort of understand it, but I can't empathize with it. To me it's just another set of irrational beliefs. You can believe this, you can believe that if you want. I don't understand why people should need irrational beliefs. Apparently many people seem to find a good deal of fulfillment in it.

**Including lots of scientists. I was quite struck by that recently finding all these physicists, chemists, biologists . . .**

Honestly, I'm pretty skeptical when I read that stuff.

**Some of those interviews are astounding.**

I remember once a close associate of Einstein's once told me, as a sort of a semi-joke, Einstein was always saying famous things . . .

**He always talks about God.**

She told me that when he says God he means "I." "God doesn't play dice with the cosmos" means "I don't believe in this stuff." When scientists talk about God and this, it reminds me a little bit of when Robert Oppenheimer used to talk about Persian poetry. One of the ways in which scientists try to look like, well, if they're not really civilized beings, the way they try to look like civilized beings is by doing things that they think are deep. Like you read Persian poetry or you think about Buddha or something like that. But that's always struck me as something of an affectation. It's striking that this kind of talk about God was not true of the generation of scientists, say, from Bohr, Planck, Max Born, and Einstein, the great period of modern science. It wasn't true. And there was a level of culture and civilization there that was real, that was not duplicated in twentieth-century America. I think this is true of a lot of things. For example, I don't think people of that generation would have named their particles "quarks," trying to show how smart they are because they read *Finnegans Wake*. They didn't have to show anybody how smart they were. They were smart and cultivated and educated. You didn't have to make everybody remember, "He read *Finnegans Wake*."

**Murray Gell-Mann is quite smart.**

"Smart" and "cultivated" are not the same thing. And it's not a matter of persons; it's a matter of the whole intellectual culture. The intellectual culture of Central Europe.

**It's also what's supported and what's not.**
The intellectual culture of Central Europe out of which a lot of this grew was qualitatively different from that of twentieth-century America.

**I recently read a book by a guy named Steven Weinberg, who's a Nobel Prize–winning physicist, very brilliant. And it is quite fascinating. The book not only makes difficult ideas accessible, but it's written in a straightforward way with no pretense. It feels wise, almost elegant in some sense.**
I knew him when he was at MIT, and I felt that.

**A lot of these guys can write that way, which you don't find coming out of the soft sciences. You won't find an economist writing a book about economics like that.**
That's true. First of all, there's not much to say. But it's certainly true. On the other hand, you were talking about the novel . . . this turning to divinity, and does the Big Bang tell us something about the creator. I think it's fairly recent in science. It's a pretty common thing. A lot of people write popular books about science now. They think you have to say that. And they didn't think they had to say it forty years ago, and that's a cultural change.

**It is a kind of different dimension, when you're talking forty, fifty years ago and you're talking about particles in the lab. Now they're talking about one-trillionth of a second after the whatever it was at the beginning.**
I don't think in terms of a conceptual revolution it's anything like the early quantum theory.

**No, it's not.**
Okay, so why didn't they say it? I think it's because they came from a different intellectual culture, where you didn't have to show that you were capable of dealing with the so-called big ideas, because you were.

**That's America.**
Yeah, I think that's twentieth-century America, a technological civilization.

**It's remarkable how religious this country is.**

It's unbelievable. It's not just that it's religious . . . if you look at the comparative studies, there's a lot of comparative studies of religious beliefs. The US is off the chart. It's like a devastated peasant society.

**If you watch TV and watch sports events where they interview people after they've done an event, regarding China you hear jokes about how they used to say, "I read Mao and he helped me jump and taught me how to do this high jump, and I won the Olympic event." But that's also the way the Americans sound, except it's God. The first thing out of their mouth is always, "I thank God."**
It's shocking, just looking at the studies, which are interesting. I was just looking at one by Andrew Greeley, which was a cross-cultural study. It turns out that 75 percent of Americans literally believe in religious miracles, for example. You can't find that anywhere else.

**But what does that mean? Deeper; what does it mean if you go up to somebody on the street and they say, I'm one of those 75 percent? What does that mean?**
Either it means that they think they have to say it or they literally believe it. Either way it's the same. It shows that there are features of the society that are off the chart with regard to industrial societies. There are other things that are striking too. There is an increasing sense that nothing is responsive to me. The institutions don't work for me at all. In fact, that figure goes higher and higher every year. It's now hitting over two-thirds of the population, which is astonishing. Eighty-three percent of the population thinks that the entire economic system is inherently unfair.

**But the two together . . . think that the economic system is unfair; they also think that there's nothing that they can do about it.**
That's why I think they're connected.

**Religion is the . . .**
That's why I say it's like a devastated peasant society. In a society where people feel they can't do anything, they turn to something supernatural. It's happening in Central America right now. The evangelical churches coming down with the story, "Don't worry about this miserable existence. It doesn't matter anyway. Things will be better later." They're gaining considerable success in the wake of murderous destruction of social reform movements.

**There's an element which makes sense. If you live under those conditions, then they're not likely to change unless you're trying to eke out the best possible existence you can, this kind of thing.**

Maybe. These are phenomena that have been looked at for a long time. Walter Dean Burnham was one of the social scientists who looked at it about ten, twelve years ago. He wrote about back to the nineteenth century there seemed to be a correlation between the lack of, say, worker organization and other popular organization in the US and the lack of political differentiation and political ideal on the one hand and the surprising degree of religious commitment on the other. It's possible that they're correlated. If you go back, there are other things to look at. The chiliastic elements in the church, millennial movements in the church, we're on the verge, the Messiah is coming, that kind of businesses, did regularly arise and was often even stimulated at times of social struggle or the collapse of social struggle.

**That's oppression.**

That kind of thing. E.P. Thompson writes about that in *The Making of the English Working Class* at the beginning of the nineteenth century. It goes right through the nineteenth century in the US. Actually . . . in fact, you see it right now in the Islamic world. Take these 415 people who were kicked out of Israel from Hamas. Israel had supported the Islamic fundamentalist movement openly, as a counterweight to secular nationalism, which is what really bothered them. They were afraid of secular nationalism which would make accommodations, proposals, they would have to deal with these issues politically, which they didn't want to do. It got to the point where they were literally shipping Islamic fundamentalist young people to break up strikes by secular nationalist students on the West Bank. Well, they got what they wanted: Islamic fundamentalists. And it's happening throughout the Arab world, the rise of Islamic fundamentalism, which people talk about as this horrible, perplexing thing. Part of it is a reaction to the failure of secular nationalism. That failure has a number of reasons, one of them being Western hostility to it. Sure, you take away people's hopes and they'll turn to something else.

**Next time we get together, perhaps we should start there, trying to work through what there is to be hopeful about, what, in more detail, is the goal we are striving for, what, in more detail, are the structures standing**

between us and that goal, and even, in more detail, what kind of activism and organization on our part might overcome those obstacles and attain the sought goals. But, for now, thank you.

# Afterword

To have met Noam Chomsky, become friends with him as a college student, and remained friends for a half century was a key factor in my life. It wasn't just learning from him and being aided by him while in school but even more thereafter. This book continues that half-century pattern.

Noam doesn't influence by charisma. He doesn't influence by force. Instead he just is, and if you are lucky enough to have the opportunity, you experience firsthand what he does and how he does it, and the example he sets influences you if you let it.

But Noam also presents information, events, and connections—in text and in speech. As his publisher we used to joke that if you want an essay from Noam, ask for a sentence. If you want a book, ask for an essay. Whatever the process, if you read his writings and hear his talks, if you really read and hear and think on it, no proximity is needed. His words influence you, if you let them.

Yes, Noam has a prodigious memory. At times it is even shocking. But the truth is, you can carry around a bigger and more exact memory in your pocket. And yes, Noam's mind maneuvers quickly and navigates complexities compellingly. True, but slow and steady wins many a race or, more relevantly, can reach the same destination.

I think what makes Noam so influential is partly his honesty, integrity, and work ethic, which together fuel the demonstration effect. He is a good example, partly because he is the archetypal antiacademic. Everything he produces is as clear as honesty permits. But I think most of all it is that for some reason Noam's mind never gets overly attached to a particular viewpoint. He always seeks better. Noam finds ways, often by a judicious and wise use of analogies, to see new relations where most of us only see what we have already seen.

Whatever contributes to him being him, Noam Chomsky is a quite special combination of mind and soul. A good example. Let him and his many offerings influence you. You will be better for it, and so will we all.

**Michael Albert**

# Index

"Passim" (literally "scattered") indicates intermittent discussion of a topic over a cluster of pages.

# About the Authors

**Noam Chomsky** is a laureate professor at the University of Arizona and professor emeritus in the MIT Department of Linguistics and Philosophy. His work is widely credited with having revolutionized the field of modern linguistics, and Chomsky is one of the foremost critics of US foreign policy. He has published numerous groundbreaking books, articles, and essays on global politics, history, and linguistics. His recent books include *Taming the Rascal Multitude* and *Between Thought and Expression Lies a Lifetime* (with James Kelman).

**Michael Albert** is an organizer, publisher, teacher, and author of over twenty books and hundreds of articles. He cofounded South End Press, *Z Magazine*, the Z Media Institute, ZNet, and various other projects, and works full time for Z Communications. He is the author of *Practical Utopia: Strategies for a Desirable Society*.

**Lydia Sargent** was a founder and original member of the South End Press Collective, as well as *Z Magazine*, which she coedited. Her plays include *I Read about My Death in Vogue Magazine* and *Playbook* with Maxine Klein and Howard Zinn. She also edited *Women and Revolution: A Discussion of the Unhappy Marriage of Marxism and Feminism*.

# ABOUT PM PRESS

PM Press is an independent, radical publisher of books and media to educate, entertain, and inspire. Founded in 2007 by a small group of people with decades of publishing, media, and organizing experience, PM Press amplifies the voices of radical authors, artists, and activists. Our aim is to deliver bold political ideas and vital stories to all walks of life and arm the dreamers to demand the impossible. We have sold millions of copies of our books, most often one at a time, face to face. We're old enough to know what we're doing and young enough to know what's at stake. Join us to create a better world.

**PM Press**
PO Box 23912
Oakland, CA 94623
www.pmpress.org

**PM Press in Europe**
europe@pmpress.org
www.pmpress.org.uk

# FRIENDS OF PM PRESS

These are indisputably momentous times—the financial system is melting down globally and the Empire is stumbling. Now more than ever there is a vital need for radical ideas.

In the years since its founding—and on a mere shoestring— PM Press has risen to the formidable challenge of publishing and distributing knowledge and entertainment for the struggles ahead. With over 450 releases to date, we have published an impressive and stimulating array of literature, art, music, politics, and culture. Using every available medium, we've succeeded in connecting those hungry for ideas and information to those putting them into practice.

*Friends of PM* allows you to directly help impact, amplify, and revitalize the discourse and actions of radical writers, filmmakers, and artists. It provides us with a stable foundation from which we can build upon our early successes and provides a much-needed subsidy for the materials that can't necessarily pay their own way. You can help make that happen—and receive every new title automatically delivered to your door once a month—by joining as a Friend of PM Press. And, we'll throw in a free T-shirt when you sign up.

Here are your options:

- **$30 a month** Get all books and pamphlets plus 50% discount on all webstore purchases

- **$40 a month** Get all PM Press releases (including CDs and DVDs) plus 50% discount on all webstore purchases

- **$100 a month** Superstar—Everything plus PM merchandise, free downloads, and 50% discount on all webstore purchases

For those who can't afford $30 or more a month, we have **Sustainer Rates** at $15, $10, and $5. Sustainers get a free PM Press T-shirt and a 50% discount on all purchases from our website.

Your Visa or Mastercard will be billed once a month, until you tell us to stop. Or until our efforts succeed in bringing the revolution around. Or the financial meltdown of Capital makes plastic redundant. Whichever comes first.

# DEPARTMENT OF ANTHROPOLOGY & SOCIAL CHANGE

Anthropology and Social Change, housed within
the California Institute of Integral Studies, is a small
innovative graduate department with a particular focus
on activist scholarship, militant research, and social change. We offer both masters
and doctoral degree programs.

Our unique approach to collaborative research methodology dissolves traditional
barriers between research and political activism, between insiders and outsiders,
and between researchers and protagonists. Activist research is a tool for "creating
the conditions we describe." We engage in the process of co-research to explore
existing alternatives and possibilities for social change.

**Anthropology and Social Change**
**anth@ciis.edu**
**1453 Mission Street**
**94103**
**San Francisco, California**
**www.ciis.edu/academics/graduate-programs/anthropology-and-social-change**

## Between Thought and Expression Lies a Lifetime: Why Ideas Matter

James Kelman & Noam Chomsky

ISBN: 978-1-62963-880-5 (paperback)
       978-1-62963-886-7 (hardcover)
$19.95/$39.95    304 pages

"The world is full of information. What do we do when we get the information, when we have digested the information, what do we do then? Is there a point where ye say, yes, stop, now I shall move on."

This exhilarating collection of essays, interviews, and correspondence—spanning the years 1988 through 2018, and reaching back a decade more—is about the simple concept that ideas matter. They mutate, inform, create fuel for thought, and inspire actions.

As Kelman says, the State relies on our suffocation, that we cannot hope to learn "the truth. But whether we can or not is beside the point. We must grasp the nettle, we assume control and go forward."

*Between Thought and Expression Lies a Lifetime* is an impassioned, elucidating, and often humorous collaboration. Philosophical and intimate, it is a call to ponder, imagine, explore, and act.

*"The real reason Kelman, despite his stature and reputation, remains something of a literary outsider is not, I suspect, so much that great, radical Modernist writers aren't supposed to come from working-class Glasgow, as that great, radical Modernist writers are supposed to be dead. Dead, and wrapped up in a Penguin Classic: that's when it's safe to regret that their work was underappreciated or misunderstood (or how little they were paid) in their lifetimes. You can write what you like about Beckett or Kafka and know they're not going to come round and tell you you're talking nonsense, or confound your expectations with a new work. Kelman is still alive, still writing great books, climbing."*
—James Meek, *London Review of Books*

*"A true original . . . A real artist. . . . It's now very difficult to see which of his peers can seriously be ranked alongside [Kelman] without ironic eyebrows being raised."*
—Irvine Welsh, *Guardian*

*"Probably the most influential novelist of the post-war period."*
—*The Times*

# Taming the Rascal Multitude: Essays, Interviews, and Lectures 1997–2014

Noam Chomsky
with an Afterword by Michael Albert

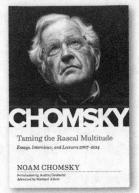

ISBN: 978-1-62963-878-2 (paperback)
978-1-62963-879-9 (hardcover)
$27.95/$59.95    448 pages

As Noam Chomsky writes about something—US foreign policy, corporate policies, an election, or a movement—he is not only quite specific in recounting the topic and its facts but also exercises blisteringly relentless logic to discern the interconnections between the evidence and broader themes involved. This may seem mundane, but virtually every time, even aside from the details of the case in question, the process, the steps, the ways of linking one thing to another illustrate what it means to be a thinking, critical subject of history and society, in any time and place.

*Taming the Rascal Multitude* is a judicious selection of essays and interviews from *Z Magazine* from 1997 to 2014. In each, Chomsky takes up some question of the moment. As such, in sum, the essays provide an historical overview of the history that preceded Trump and the reaction to Trump. The essays situate what followed even without having known what would follow. They explicate what preceded the current era and provide a step-by-step revelation or how-to for successfully comprehending social events and relations. They are a pleasure to read, much like the pleasure of watching a great athlete or performer, but they also edify. They educate.

Reading Chomsky is about understanding how society works, how people relate to society and social trends and patterns and why, and, beyond the specifics, how to approach events, relations, occurrences, trends, and patterns in a way that reveals their inner meanings and their outer connections and implications. It is like reading the best you can get about topic after topic, and, more, it is like watching a master-craftsmen in a discipline that ought to be all of ours understanding the world to change it.

*"Noam Chomsky is the world's most humane, philosophically sophisticated, and knowledgeable public intellectual. "*
—Richard Falk, professor of international law emeritus, Princeton University

*"Chomsky is a global phenomenon. . . . He may be the most widely read American voice on foreign policy on the planet."*
—New York Times Book Review

## Yugoslavia: Peace, War, and Dissolution

Noam Chomsky. Edited by Davor Džalto with a Preface by Andrej Grubačić

ISBN: 978-1-62963-442-5
$19.95    240 pages

The Balkans, in particular the turbulent ex-Yugoslav territory, have been among the most important world regions in Noam Chomsky's political reflections and activism for decades. His articles, public talks, and correspondence have provided a critical voice on political and social issues crucial not only to the region but the entire international community, including "humanitarian intervention," the relevance of international law in today's politics, media manipulations, and economic crisis as a means of political control.

This volume provides a comprehensive survey of virtually all of Chomsky's texts and public talks that focus on the region of the former Yugoslavia, from the 1970s to the present. With numerous articles and interviews, this collection presents a wealth of materials appearing in book form for the first time along with reflections on events twenty-five years after the official end of communist Yugoslavia and the beginning of the war in Bosnia. The book opens with a personal and wide-ranging preface by Andrej Grubačić that affirms the ongoing importance of Yugoslav history and identity, providing a context for understanding Yugoslavia as an experiment in self-management, antifascism, and multiethnic coexistence.

*"Chomsky is a global phenomenon. . . . He may be the most widely read American voice on foreign policy on the planet."*
—New York Times Book Review

*"For anyone wanting to find out more about the world we live in... there is one simple answer: read Noam Chomsky."*
—New Statesman

*"With relentless logic, Chomsky bids us to listen closely to what our leaders tell us—and to discern what they are leaving out. . . . Agree with him or not, we lose out by not listening."*
—Businessweek

# Practical Utopia: Strategies for a Desirable Society

Michael Albert
with a preface by Noam Chomsky

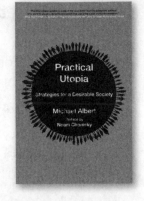

ISBN: 978-1-62963-381-7
$20.00     288 pages

Michael Albert's latest work, *Practical Utopia* is a succinct and thoughtful discussion of ambitious goals and practical principles for creating a desirable society. It presents concepts and their connections to current society; visions of what can be in a preferred, participatory future; and an examination of the ends and means required for developing a just society. Neither shying away from the complexity of human issues, nor reeking of dogmatism, *Practical Utopia* presupposes only concern for humanity.

Part one offers conceptual tools for understanding society and history, for discerning the nature of the oppressions people suffer and the potentials they harbor. Part two promotes a vision for a better way of organizing economy, polity, kinship, culture, ecology, and international relations. It is not a blueprint, of course, but does address the key institutions needed if people are to be free to determine their own circumstances. Part three investigates the means of seeking change using a variety of tactics and programs.

"*Practical Utopia immediately struck me because it is written by a leftist who is interested in the people winning and defeating oppression. The book is an excellent jumping off point for debates on the framework to look at actually existing capitalism, strategy for change, and what we need to do about moving forward. It speaks to many of the questions faced by grassroots activists who want to get beyond demanding change but who, instead, want to create a dynamic movement that can bring a just world into existence. As someone who comes out of a different part of the Left than does Michael Albert, I was nevertheless excited by the challenges he threw in front of the readers of this book. Many a discussion will be sparked by the arguments of this work.*"
—Bill Fletcher Jr., author of *"They're Bankrupting Us!" And 20 Other Myths about Unions*

"*Albert mulls over the better society that we may create after capitalism, provoking much thought and offering a generous, hopeful vision of the future. Albert's prescriptions for action in the present are modest and wise, his suggestions for building the future are ambitious and humane.*"
—Milan Rai